# WHY VIBES MATTER

WELBECK
BALANCE

# WHY VIBES MATTER

Garret Yount

WELBECK
BALANCE

Published in 2023 by Welbeck Balance
An imprint of Welbeck Non-Fiction Limited
Part of Welbeck Publishing Group
Offices in: London – 20 Mortimer Street, London W1T 3JW &
Sydney – 205 Commonwealth Street, Surry Hills 2010
www.welbeckpublishing.com

A CIP catalogue record for this book is available from the British Library.

ISBN
978-1-80129-274-0

Typeset by Lapiz Digital Services
Printed in Great Britain by CPI Group (UK) Ltd, Croydon CRO 4YY

10 9 8 7 6 5 4 3 2 1

MIX
Paper | Supporting
responsible forestry
FSC® C171272

# ABOUT THE AUTHOR

Garret Yount, PhD, is a scientist and molecular biologist at the Institute of Noetic Sciences where his research focuses on mapping the mind-gene interface. He obtained his BS from the Department of Molecular & Cell Biology at the Pennsylvania State University, and his PhD from the Department of Neurobiology & Behavior at the State University of New York at Stony Brook. Dr Yount has a long-standing interest in developing methods and technologies for bridging molecular neurobiology with aspects of consciousness. He has conducted carefully controlled laboratory experiments with spiritual healers and biofield practitioners from around the world, including China, Brazil, Canada, USA, Japan, India, Russia, Hungary and Sri Lanka.

# CONTENTS

# INTRODUCTION

Max Plank, the Nobel Prize winner credited with the birth of quantum physics, famously said: "All the physical matters are composed of vibration."

The truth is that we are all made up of vibrations. Every object in the universe vibrates. Even though it feels solid and still, this book is vibrating. If you get really technical about it, you are not even actually touching it. The electron waves of all the atoms in the book repel the electron waves on the surface of your hands. These vibrating energy waves are the foundation of our entire reality.

## *What do we mean by vibes?*

These energy vibes referred to by Plank are only part of the story. Long before the birth of quantum physics, or even classical physics, people described energies and forces – "life force energy" – in religious texts from ancient India, forces that affect our bodies and minds but that can't be measured by scientific instruments. I'll refer to these unseen forces throughout the book as "subtle energy vibes."

In disparate cultures across the globe, subtle energy vibes are accepted as part of everyday life, compared to the West where this is often viewed as something "other" or "out there." Qi (pronounced "chee") is a life force energy described in ancient Chinese texts and remains an important concept in modern China that informs daily decisions, such as choosing to drink warm water rather than adding ice to it because of the belief that coldness can interfere with the flow of qi in the stomach and spleen. Subtle energies such as qi are believed to be the basis of healing modalities that have been practiced throughout history in virtually every known culture (Rubik, et al., 2015), from the doshas of Indian Ayurveda and reflexology from Ancient Egypt to Hindu chakra practices and Japanese Reiki (a form of energy healing).

Taking qi as the example, qigong is a health-promoting practice stemming from Traditional Chinese Medicine (TCM) based on the mental manipulation of the qi. Qigong practice involves meditative techniques for balancing the flow of qi in our bodies to recover from illnesses and maintain good health. TCM defines qi as a "life force energy permeating our bodies" and posits that blockages or imbalances of the flow of qi are what cause illness. These techniques are based on the foundational TCM tenet stating, "where thought goes, qi goes," and we'll look more at the idea of the power of intention and vibes later.

## *What are examples of vibes?*

Here in the West, the word "vibes" can mean so many different things. We often describe "vibes" as an unexplainable strange feeling or sensation that can be positive or negative – we've all had "that" feeling – we've felt our mood shift (positively or negatively) when meeting a stranger for the first time, or sensed an "atmosphere" when we've walked into a room, or noticed positivity radiating from someone. There is a distinct quality that connects all of these experiences – a sensory and energy shift that's often called "vibes." Perhaps we've had "a feeling" about something – prompting us to change our plans, to call an old friend, or to take a different route in life. These vibes affect us, they steer our life choices and influence how we relate to those around us, and this subtle energy can also be used in healing and to balance the body.

## *The Institute of Noetic Sciences*

The modern scientific investigation of these subtle energy vibes and their manipulation has only begun relatively recently. I have had the privilege of pioneering some of the research, most recently as part of a team at the Institute of Noetic Sciences (IONS). The term "noetic" refers to our inner space, and our ability to tune in to information on a feeling level, rather than an intellectual level. IONS was founded by the Apollo astronaut Edgar Mitchell after he had an epiphany as he looked at Earth from space.

> *"Instead of an intellectual search, there was suddenly a very deep gut feeling that something was different. It occurred when looking at Earth and seeing this blue-and-white planet floating there . . . knowing for sure – that there was a purposefulness of flow, of energy, of time, of space in the cosmos – that it was beyond man's rational ability to understand . . ."*

My research has focused on subtle energy vibes in the context of healing. I've conducted controlled experiments with traditional healers from around the world, including China, Brazil, Canada, USA, Japan, India, Russia, Hungary and Sri Lanka. I have included some of these experiments in the book, along with compelling findings from other scientific experiments examining all kinds of vibes.

# *Where do vibes come from?*

*Why Vibes Matter* explores a myriad of vibes and their sources. Many vibes that we emit and experience every day are **conscious vibes**, the emotional signals we broadcast to and receive from those around us – for example, smiling or frowning at somebody. The ambience of a place is also a conscious vibe. When a couple decides on a rustic vibe for their wedding, they are creating an atmosphere that their guests will notice and respond to, thinking about the simplicity of country life, and the beauty of nature. These vibes are reactions to our conscious perceptions.

I am not going to dwell on conscious vibes in this book. Instead, I'll focus on what I'll call **subconscious vibes** – "invisible" vibes that well up from our subconscious mind and have a powerful influence on how we act in a given situation, making them an extremely significant part of our hidden psychology.

Subconscious vibes often show up as a feeling and we don't always know why we feel that way – it could be a response to a person who seems irrational or an instinct to do something or go somewhere that comes without obvious reason. Our senses can be a source of these vibes. Seeing different colors, for example, can affect our mood subconsciously, and drive our snap judgements about buying things. "Unconscious somatic influences" are another source of vibes that I'll discuss – these are our bodies' physiological reactions to stimuli that our senses don't detect, like odorless gas in the environment or even the chemicals released from another person's sweat or tears (often called biophysical vibes). It has also been shown that our bodies can react to the electromagnetic field emanating from another person's body nearby. I'll even discuss the fascinating experiments around scopaesthesia, the name given to that strange sensation you get when you know someone is staring at you. There's also the belief that people can "leave behind" energy in certain places to be felt by others, plus examples of haunted places and sites that seem imbued with a special energy.

## *People and places*

I have divided the book into two parts. Part One is devoted to vibes relating to and involving other **people**, such as the vibes we get when we meet a person and immediately get a feeling about them, or when it seems as if you are vibrating on the same frequency with another person, and other similar inter- and intrapersonal experiences.

Part Two discusses vibes associated with **places**, ranging from the stressed-out feeling caused by messy tables and cluttered and cramped rooms in your home to sensing the spiritual vibes of a sacred place of ceremony or ritual, like standing in a church or on a historic site and sensing an atmosphere charged with a spiritual energy.

## How to use this book

*Why Vibes Matter* is an illuminating guide to using your energy wisely and understanding the "hidden messages" you are picking up. There are many remarkable claims related to vibes buzzing around in popular culture and exploring the science and research behind the theories gives us some mind-blowing gold nuggets amongst a lot of urban myths. I've picked out some of the riches to share with you here.

I've included practical tools and techniques in each chapter to help you to interact with vibes in a positive way. Some methods are about influencing and altering the vibes around you, such as smudging your house with herbs, while others are designed to help you to tune in to your subconscious vibes and tap into your body's subtle energy more clearly, such as meditative practices.

Whatever stage of spiritual evolution or exploration you are at, this is powerful stuff. The practices can have real effects on your body, so your health provider should know what you're up to, especially if you are trying a method as part of a self-healing journey.

I feel honored to be able to spread the word about these practices because I believe that our capacity for self-knowledge and self-healing is vastly underappreciated. And this is just one of the many reasons why vibes matter. I invite you to explore with me and discover the unlimited potential of your vibes, opening yourself up to the idea of the vibrations underlying all aspects of reality connecting everything. Shall we begin?

# PART 1
# PEOPLE

Have you ever met someone and immediately had a feeling about them? Getting a vibe or an instinctive response when you meet a new person is common. Sometimes we express it as feeling we're "on the same wavelength" as another person. It is also common to have a "gut feeling" about somebody we've just met. Vibes like these matter because they guide and change our thoughts and behaviors toward these new people. Perhaps we go out of our way to help a new work colleague as we feel a kinship with them, or we accept or reject an invitation to grab a coffee with someone new based on how we instinctively feel about them on a brief meeting.

In this part of the book, we explore some of the varied ways that people experience vibes associated with people. We will look at:

- Getting a vibe when you meet a person
- Being "at one" with another person
- Having a "psychic" connection with a loved one in distress
- The feeling of being stared at

We'll examine contributing factors to why we feel vibes with other people and highlight some fascinating research studies related to these experiences. I'll also describe some techniques designed to harness this energy for healing and becoming more self-aware, ranging from the right way to chant "Om" to practices that focus on creating a deep, intimate connection with others.

# CHAPTER 1

---

## GETTING A VIBE WHEN YOU MEET SOMEONE

Most of us instinctively make judgements of others when we meet someone new. Often these quick assessments are just part of our ongoing inner commentary about what is happening as we navigate the day – for me, it can sometimes sound like a panel of sports commentators sussing up a new player that runs onto the playing field – but sometimes our reaction to a new person comes through with a little extra oomph. In this case, the body gets the feeling first. Psychologists have labeled the source for this type of reaction as "unconscious somatic influences" (Lufityanto, et al., 2016), i.e., these are unconscious responses triggered by our physical body.

These subconscious vibes stem from the nervous system, the control center of the body and coordinator of all messaging from the sensory organs. The nervous system can detect and react to signals in our environment before the conscious mind gets the memo – changing our blood pressure, heart rate and breathing, for example – and we'll review some science that uncovers how this feels for us. I'll share two simple techniques – slowing down your breathing and chanting – for raising the frequency of the vibes you are experiencing as well as sending out for others to pick up.

## *Implicit biases are not vibes*

To begin with, know that first impressions can be susceptible to manipulations, they depend very much on what kind of signals a person, consciously and unconsciously, is sending out to be picked up on. They're also very dependent on how your mind is receiving those signals. The way that new person appears, how they dress, their body movements, etc. are all filtered through the lens of the stuff going on in your mind. This lens includes your attitudes toward specific groups of people. I mentioned this because, if you only pay attention to the information coming through that lens, you run the risk of allowing implicit biases to dominate your decisions about a new person.

Implicit biases are attitudes that may have been learned during your upbringing or acquired through experiences with individuals from certain groups. I was shocked to learn that implicit biases often predict how we'll react to a stranger more accurately than a list of the values we say that we believe in. This was shown in a meta-analysis of 122 studies of stereotyping and prejudice by Anthony Greenwald and colleagues at the University of Washington in Seattle. The studies reviewed in the meta-analysis involved a total of nearly 15,000 participants, and showed that implicit biases measured with the Implicit Association Test (the most commonly used reaction time measure for implicit biases) better predict behavior than explicit self-reports (Greenwald, et al., 2009). For example, stereotypes such as associating weapons more strongly with black people than white people can predict real-world behavior such as how job candidates are evaluated and how people are treated as patients.

Since implicit biases exist below our conscious awareness, figuring out whether they are influencing your behavior in any given situation is tricky. To get a better understanding of this conundrum, I recommend a book written by Jonathan Haidt titled *The Righteous Mind: Why Good People Are Divided by Politics and Religion* (Haidt, 2013), because he does a great job of describing how our conscious mind has a habit of rationalizing – after the fact – whatever we do on impulse.

## *Do I smell?*

Fortunately, a person's appearance is not the only type of information available to us when we encounter someone. Chemicals emitted from our bodies, such as hormones in our sweat or tears and miscellaneous body odors, can trigger unconscious responses in people around us. Of these biophysical vibes or biophysical mechanisms, pheromones are the most famous example of this source of subconscious vibes. Pheromones are chemicals emitted to waft through the air between animals of the same species, influencing behavior by, for example, causing hormonal changes. They're unseen subconscious signals or communications that sometimes cannot even be detected by smell.

Some of the most striking evidence for the effects of pheromones have been found by scientists studying rodents. Young female rats enter puberty earlier when they are exposed to adult male rats, for example. This early blooming is due to pheromones emitted by the males and inhaled by the females (Kennedy and Brown, 1970). In another study, researchers at the Massachusetts Institute of Technology observed that male hamsters will mount and attempt to copulate with other males that are knocked out with anesthesia and perfumed with female hamster vaginal discharge (Murphy, 1973). I'm not going to claim that hamsters are picking up subconscious vibes the way that we do, but you've got to admit that it's pretty impressive how a chemical signal can drive behavior in this way.

The story of pheromones in humans is a little more intriguing; scientists are still not sure whether or not we really have them (Wyatt, 2015). Most of the chemicals that are contenders for being human pheromones are secreted in armpit sweat. Reports of this in the popular media led some men to believe that their sweat is an aphrodisiac. I mentioned this to my wife and received a hearty guffaw.

In my defense, there is a nugget of truth in the idea. One of the chemicals in armpit sweat that seems to function as a pheromone – called androstadienone – is described as having an unpleasant or pleasant odor, depending on who you ask (Jacob et al., 2006). Researchers at the University of Liverpool tested the effects of androstadienone in experiments designed to mimic a speed-dating event. They recruited women and men who had never met before and shuffled them around, allowing the various couples to spend three minutes talking with each other. The women were asked to score the attractiveness of the potential date while they had a cotton wool pad taped under their noses containing either androstadienone in 1% clove oil, just 1% clove oil, or water. The results found that men were rated more attractive when assessed by the women inhaling androstadienone (Saxton, et al., 2008).

## *The "smell" of women's tears*

Armpits don't have a monopoly on excreting chemicals that can trigger unconscious vibes. Researchers at the Weizmann Institute of Science in Israel collected tears from women while they were watching a sad movie and asked men to sniff the tears. The men reported being "turned off" sexually after sniffing the tears compared to those sniffing just salt water (Gelstein, et al., 2011).

The idea that pheromone-like chemicals could be produced in tears is not completely out of left field. Again, pioneering studies were done with rodents. Researchers at the University of Tokyo showed that the tears of rats contain something that their "cousins" – mice – can detect and which affects the behavior of mice when inhaled (Tsunoda, et al., 2018). A fact about rats that may surprise you (it did me) is that rats are predators of mice. This predator–prey relationship seems to explain the effect that rat tears have on mice. When the mice detected molecules in the air from rat tears through receptors in their noses, they automatically went "as quiet as church mice." They became still and their body temperatures and heart rates dropped, making them harder to find.

Knowing that our mammalian cousins send signals with their tears is what inspired the group in Israel to look for some kind of tear-based signaling in humans. They were interested in tears produced from crying rather than the actual tear films (the "tear" layer in the eye), since crying with emotion is a uniquely human thing to do. The scientists hypothesized that sad tears would decrease men's libido, since that seems to be the general effect from field studies of couples in their natural habitat. In the experiment, men sniffed an odorless liquid and then looked at photos of random women's faces, which they rated for sadness and sexual attractiveness. The researchers didn't tell the men what the experiment was about, and the men never saw the women, let alone observed them crying (confirming that they were studying something beyond just emotional reactions). The liquid they sniffed was either "sad tears" or salt water (salt water being the control condition in this experiment, allowing the researchers to filter out any reactions not related to the specific variable being tested and draw conclusions from the data). To be extra careful not to accidentally signal anything to the men, the researchers presenting the liquids were also kept in the dark about which type of liquid was being used. When the men rated the random photos, there was no difference in how they rated the sadness of the faces when they were sniffing either sad tears or salt water (so there is no "sadness signal" carried in tears) but there was a significant drop in how they rated their sexual arousal when viewing the photos after sniffing tears but not salt water.

This cold shower effect of some odorless component of tears was so provocative that these researchers repeated the study looking for evidence that the men were being affected at the physiological level, and they hit the jackpot. Not only did the men report that they felt less aroused when sniffing women's tears, it was found that the level of testosterone in their blood decreased, and brain-imaging revealed less activity in the parts of the brain associated with sexual arousal. All that, just from the smell of tears!

## *Smelling a friend*

Recently, the researchers at the Weizmann Institute of Science have moved their smelling research into the "friend" zone. They built an electronic sniffer to carry on their research on nose-based signaling by humans. This time they tested the hypothesis that when humans subconsciously smell themselves and others – which we do a lot – we make subconscious comparisons and gravitate toward people whose smell is similar to our own. The people recruited for this study were either pairs of non-romantic friends whose friendships had originally formed very rapidly, referred to as "click friends," or pairs of random strangers. The researchers collected body odor samples from both pair groups and tested whether the electronic sniffer could tell the difference (Ravreby, et al., 2022). The answer was a resounding yes. The electronic sniffer determined that the click friends had a body odor signature that was much more similar than that of the random pairs.

The researchers anticipated the criticism that these results might be caused by some lifestyle choices that the click friends started to have in common as a result of their friendship. Maybe they had decided to try a vegan diet together prompting their body odor signatures to be more similar now. To address this potential criticism, the researchers recruited a group of strangers for the electronic sniffer to sniff and tested whether it could *predict* which ones might be "click friends" material. After providing body odor samples, these complete strangers were asked to pair off and do exercises together that involved nonverbal social interactions. After spending time together, each individual rated their partner in terms of how much they liked that person and how likely they were to become friends. According to the electronic sniffer, the pairs who had more positive interactions smelled more like each other.

This supports the likelihood that vibes coming from our bodies through subconscious biophysical signals such as our hormones contribute to who we spend our time with and form relationships with – both platonic and romantic. When we instinctively "warm to" others and connect strongly, we believe it's a conscious decision based on what that person has told us and who they are, but the reality is much more nuanced.

## The body's electromagnetic field (EMF) and vibes

Let's move on from unseen chemical communications to another form of hidden energy signaling. Electromagnetic fields (EMFs) are generated whenever an electric current is flowing and can be either natural or human-made. They consist of waves of vibrating electric and magnetic fields – as more electric current flows, the strength of a magnetic field increases. The Earth has an EMF, generated from electric currents caused by flowing liquid metal below the surface of the planet. Our bodies also have multiple EMFs because our brains and muscles generate electric current when they're operating (Cohen, et al., 1980). Just to be clear, this is different from being magnetized. (Metal objects won't start sticking to you if you think really hard or flex your muscles like a bodybuilder.) An EMF is more like an invisible area of low-level radiation coming from the body that can be detected by sensitive instruments in a lab, and the body's EMF is weaker than the Earth's because the electric current flowing in our bodies is puny compared to that of the planet.

The strength of the body's EMFs are determined to a large extent by the muscle mass and nerves that supply the muscle fibers, and the heart is the most powerful source of an EMF in the human body. The heart's EMF is more than a hundred times stronger than the brain's and it can be detected up to three feet away from the body, in all directions, using a very sensitive magnetometer called a superconducting quantum interference device (SQUID). When the field is visualized, it looks like an inflated donut shape surrounding the body. The heart's EMF can also be measured on the surface of the body in the form of an electrocardiogram, which uses electrodes placed on the skin to record the electrical activity of the heart.

Researchers at the HeartMath Institute in Boulder Creek, California, used the electrocardiogram to measure the heart EMF of people experiencing different emotions and discovered evidence that a person's emotional state is reflected in the EMF (McCraty, 2003). They showed this by first measuring the heart EMF of people while they were in a state of deep gratitude. The squiggly lines that the electrocardiogram produced had a certain pattern. Then the scientists compared that pattern to the pattern produced while the same people were recalling feelings of anger. The patterns were different. They found that the squiggly lines were less chaotic when people were experiencing deep gratitude. Incredibly then, scientists can observe and measure the field of electromagnetic energy surrounding the body associated with different emotional states. If you're brimming with positive emotions, it shows up in the patterns of your EMF – you are literally radiating good vibes because of the EMF's waves of vibrating electric and magnetic fields. This is one way you can achieve "higher" vibrations (more about this in the next chapter).

A second extraordinary discovery the HeartMath group made was that these biophysical vibes can also affect those around them. Research showed that the heart EMF of one person can transfer energy to the that of another person. They detected this energy transfer by noticing patterns in the EMF of one person reflected in the EMF of another nearby person. Imagine that someone you meet is angry. Their EMF pattern reflects this anger and when your EMF begins to overlap with theirs – as the invisible, donut-shaped vibrating fields overlap – their EMF can transfer some "angry energy pattern" to your EMF and this impact seeps up to your conscious mind as a bad vibe. I consider this such a significant breakthrough because it provides a plausible scientific explanation, based on conventional biophysical principles and demonstrated on standard scientific instruments, for a way in which we are able to pick up subtle moods and invisible responses (subconscious vibes) from another person. If you combine the connection between emotional states and patterns representing in the EMF with the ability of the EMF to transfer energy to another person's EMF, it's easy to imagine how emotional states could be picked up by the other person at a subconscious level through the interactions of their EMFs. Suddenly, the time you spend surrounded by positive people feels more important and you realize the impact of, say, constant interactions with negative work colleagues and their toll.

## *The body's EMF and biofield therapies*

In addition to providing a potential mechanism for picking up vibes from another person, the breakthrough discoveries by the HeartMath group may also provide a potential mechanism for how biofield therapies, like qigong and Reiki, work – at least in part.

Their experiments did not investigate biofield healers but if you consider that *emotional states* can cause changes in EMF patterns that can be transferred to another person's EMF, it is a reasonable guess that *intentional states*, like the intention to heal, might also cause changes in the EMF that could be transferred.

There have been conflicting results from studies testing out this hunch. One of the well-designed studies testing this supposition was performed at the Scripps Institute in San Diego and it did not yield any convincing evidence that practicing Reiki produces changes in the EMF (Baldwin, et al., 2013). This study used SQUID to measure the EMF from the hands and heart area of three Reiki masters when they were (1) not practicing Reiki, (2) sending Reiki to a distant person, and (3) sending Reiki to a person in the room. The Scripps group noticed something going on in the EMFs of two of the Reiki masters – an extra vibration, as it were – but it was present under all conditions, even when there was no Reiki happening.

Regardless of whether or not future studies reveal evidence that EMFs can justify the effects of biofield therapies, EMFs would not be able to explain *all* of the effects of biofield therapies that have been reported. For example, they would not be able to mediate the nonlocal effects of some therapies, because EMFs are known to fade with distance. In the HeartMath study, the transfer of energy between the "donut radiation fields" was only evident when people were touching or positioned close to each other. It faded as they got further apart and was not detectable when subjects were separated by a distance of four feet. This dissipation is expected for an EMF because waves of vibrating electric and magnetic fields are supposed to lose power as they travel farther and farther away.

In contrast, qi and other esoteric forms of energy that are the basis of biofield therapy traditions are believed to exert their effects independent of distance.

## *Let scientists be scientists*

I expect that scientists will be chipping away at these questions for years to come. Meanwhile, you're free to have your own direct experience of qigong and Reiki and other biofield therapies without being able to explain it scientifically. If you ever doubt that, just remember that scientists can't yet explain what gravity "is" in any fundamental way. They only know how it behaves, which is not so different from the biofield practitioners that have studied how qi and other subtle energies behave, in some cases for thousands of years.

I don't worry about how qigong works when I'm not in the lab. When I'm practicing qigong meditation, I can feel sensations and I experience benefits.

Anybody can do the same. According to the sages, whenever you start to feel something, whether it feels like a vibration, a tingling or any other pleasant and surprising sensation, that is "it."

Next, I'll share two simple methods to enable you to feel good vibes, and experience the accompanying physiological effects, maximizing your chances that others will pick up good vibes from you, helping you to make "good" connections with those around you.

## *Slow down your breath to send good vibes*

Let's dive into one of my favourite meditation practices for "raising your vibrations." I introduce this here because it's one way to be sure that you're sending good vibes out to other people. As we've seen, the subconscious vibes you pick up from somebody are a helpful way to augment your first impression as you access more information than you glean from just their appearance and body language. On the flip side, paying attention to the subconscious vibes you are putting out can also help you to make a better first impression on others.

Maximize your chances of sending out good vibes by quieting your mind and calming your emotions. One of the methods that I find very effective for this is deep, slow breathing. Some cool science has been done around breath control and you won't be surprised to hear that there is plenty of evidence that breathing exercises are beneficial to health and wellbeing (see below), but they don't agree on *how* it works. Let's start with how to do it.

## *Step-by-step slow-breathing exercise*

1. Start your slow-breathing exercise by getting comfortable in a position in which your chest and belly are not cramped, either lying down, sitting or standing.
2. Bring your attention to your breath and try to even out the timing of your inhalations and exhalations (don't worry about being exact).
3. Count in your head to see how many counts it takes to breathe in and how many to breathe out. This is your own starting rate.
4. Begin to slow down the breath by adding one beat to your starting rate and breathing in and out at that rate for the next few breaths. For example, if you started with a breathing rate of two counts for inhaling and two counts for exhaling, then stretch the next breath out so

that it takes three counts for each inhalation and exhalation.

5.  Once you've become accustomed to the new, slower breathing rate, you can either continue breathing like that for as long as you like or stretch it out further by increasing the count by one again.

6.  For most people, getting to a count of four in and four out is the sweet spot.

Aside from trying a specific slow-breathing exercise, you can also simply slow your breath while you are going about your day. It is not mandatory to have a specific technique. Simply start breathing more slowly to experience the benefits of slow breathing. Unless there is a reason to breathe quickly, such as you need to sprint to catch a bus or something, then go with slow.

## *Breath rate and longevity*

It would be easy to doubt that something as simple as changing how you breathe could really matter. Interestingly, there is a striking correlation between the breath rate and how long animals live. Consider the tortoise. Tortoises can live for over 200 years, and they take three to four breaths per minute. We take an average of 12 breaths per minute, which is about three times as fast as the tortoise, and our average age expectancy is around 70 years. So, tortoises breathe about three times slower than us and live about three times longer than us. Dogs live around 12 years and take about 22 breaths per minute. So, they breathe around twice as fast as us and have a lifespan about six times shorter than ours. Mice breathe about ten times as fast as us and they have a lifespan of one to two years, which is around 50 times shorter than ours.

Slower breathing correlates to longer lives and there are plenty of studies that provide hints as to how slow breathing could lead to better health and longer life. One important link is between slow breathing and balanced autonomic function, the preservation of which has been linked to longevity (Zulfiqar, et al., 2010). Autonomic function refers to the activity of the autonomic nervous system – the part of your overall nervous system that controls the *automatic* processes of your body. These are physiological processes you don't think about, such as heart rate, blood pressure, digestion and sexual arousal. The autonomic nervous system is divided into three branches: the sympathetic, parasympathetic and enteric nervous systems. We'll talk more about the enteric nervous system, sometimes called the "gut brain," later in Chapter 4, but for now let me briefly explain the sympathetic and parasympathetic nervous systems as they relate to health and longevity.

The sympathetic nervous system is a network of nerves that activates systems in the body necessary to respond to an event perceived as stressful or frightening. This acute stress response prepares the body to fight or flee. The parasympathetic nervous system is a network of nerves that relaxes the body after periods of stress or danger. It is in charge of running life-sustaining processes and restores the body to ordinary functions. Popular rhymes used to contrast these two branches of the autonomic nervous system are "fight or flight" for the sympathetic nervous system and "rest and digest" or "feed and breed" for the parasympathetic branch. The balance of these two branches is essential for living a long, healthy life.

## *Slow breathing to balance autonomic function*

Sadly, modern humans tend to push the "fight or flight" branch into overdrive. Unlike our distant ancestors who activated their sympathetic nervous system sparingly – for example, to survive the infrequent saber-tooth tiger attack – modern humans activate it frequently, almost literally "at the drop of a hat." The list of events that many of us perceive as stressful or frightening seems endless and relentless. An event as trivial as somebody cutting in front of you at the grocery store, if this causes you to lose your temper, activates your sympathetic nervous system. Worrying about an event that happened in the past can also activate your sympathetic nervous system, as can worrying about something that may or may not happen in the future. The result is a loss of balance between sympathetic and parasympathetic nervous system activity, with severely diminished life-sustaining processes by the parasympathetic branch. This imbalance is a major risk factor for the development and progression of a number of diseases, including cardiovascular disease, cancer, arthritis, and major depression (Muscatell and Eisenberger, 2012). The good news is that slow breathing can help to restore this balance.

Investigations into the physiological effects of slow breathing have shown significant effects that contribute to restoring a healthy balance between the sympathetic and parasympathetic nervous systems (Russo, et al., 2017). As one example, researchers at Nepal Medical College in Kathmandu evaluated the immediate effects on heart rate and blood pressure of slowing breathing for five minutes (Pramanik, et al., 2009). Healthy volunteers were asked to sit comfortably on a fairly soft seat placed on the floor, keeping their head, neck and trunk erect, eyes closed, and the other muscles reasonably loose as they slowed their breathing down to six breaths per minute (about a count of four in and four out). During the practice the volunteers were asked not to think too much about their breathing but rather to imagine the open blue sky. The results were fantastic: after just a short period, the heart rate and blood pressure measurements showed "a strong tendency to improving the autonomic nervous system through enhanced activation of the parasympathetic system."

Another study that looked at the longer-term effects of slow breathing was conducted by researchers in India at the Jawaharlal Institute of Postgraduate Medical Education and Research Pondicherry (Pal, et al., 2004). This study divided a group of 60 volunteers into two groups: a slow-breathing group (practicing slow-breathing exercises) and a fast-breathing group (practicing fast-breathing exercises). The breathing exercises were completed for a period of three months, after which autonomic function tests were performed. The results showed decreased sympathetic activity and increased parasympathetic activity in the slow-breathing group, but no significant change in autonomic function in the fast-breathing group.

## The right way to chant "Om"

Claims of the health-enhancing effects of slow breathing are not new. Pranayama is an ancient breath technique that originates from spiritual practices in India, often performed in conjunction with meditation or yoga, and it has been associated with numerous beneficial health effects (Jayawardena, et al., 2020). It involves controlling your breath in different ways, and slow-breathing features in many of the techniques. Another style of pranayama breath control is rhythmic breathing while vocalizing, or chanting. Chanting is one of my favourite simple methods for quieting the mind, and therefore being in the best position for your body to send out positive vibes. Chanting is effective as it gives your mind something to do, with the advantage that your breath is controlled without you needing to think about it at all.

My favourite way to do it is chanting the word "Om." The word Om is defined by Hindu scripture as being the primordial sound of creation; it is believed to be the original vibration of the universe, and from this first vibration all other vibrations are able to manifest. The way it is spelled is a little deceptive – it is sometimes spelled "AUM," which is a more helpful spelling for pronunciation, and it may be helpful to think of it as "AAA-UUU-MMM" when you're chanting.

To start, get into any comfortable standing, sitting or lying position, as long as your chest and belly are not cramped. When you're ready to begin, close your eyes and start uttering the word Om with every out-breath, beginning with the mouth wide open to pronounce the first syllable "AAA". As you continue to breathe out, slowly allow your mouth to close without moving your tongue. As your mouth closes, the second syllables "UUU" and "MMM" will naturally come out. It is that simple.

Here are some bonus tips:

- Be sure to let your breathing rhythm determine the timing of the chant. In other words, don't try to fit your breathing to the chant.
- Open up your imagination to feeling the sound create vibrations in your body.
- Keep repeating the sounds with each breath for as long as you like. Usually, it takes at least three times for me to start to really feel the vibrations ramping up.
- Ideally, when you finish chanting, breathe normally and spend five minutes focusing your awareness on the breath. When your mind wanders or starts up the internal chatter, as it will, simply acknowledge that it did and return your attention to your breath.

These are the steps for chanting Om as I remember learning them from Swami Satya Brahmananda at the Universal Yoga Center in San Francisco. I was fortunate to learn this practice from this unique teacher, a scholar of Hindu philosophy and also a retired Electrical Engineering professor from Stanford University. If you enjoy this exercise and want to explore it deeply, I advise you to find a coach or adept teacher of spiritual practices of Hinduism, Buddhism or Jainism.

## SUMMARY

We've learned much about swapping personal vibes with those close to us – what is happening below our conscious awareness . . .

- Chemicals emitted from your body
  (e.g., sweat, tears) can trigger unconscious responses in others, even if they can't sense them – this is an example of subconscious vibes or unconscious somatic influences. These subconscious vibes can influence a range of reactions, including how we're feeling, how attracted we are to others, and who we gravitate toward and/or bond with quickly.
- Our emotional state is reflected in patterns in our EMF that spread vibes to those around us – we can literally radiate happiness.

- EMFs provide a plausible scientific explanation, based on conventional biophysical principles and demonstrated on standard scientific instruments, for a way in which we are able to pick up on subtle/invisible responses and subconscious vibes from others close to us.
- There are simple positive steps we can take to improve the vibes we send out. As a result, a good way to be sure that you're sending good vibes out to people is to raise your own vibes, with simple techniques like slow breathing and chanting.
- A calm mind and positive emotions correspond with higher vibes, and vice versa.
- Investigations into the physiological effects of slow breathing have uncovered evidence that it can rebalance autonomic nervous system function, essential to health and longevity.
- Slow-breathing techniques don't need to be complicated – they can be as simple as just breathing a little more slowly while chanting as an easy way to achieve slow breathing without needing to think about it.

# CHAPTER 2

---

# BEING "IN TUNE"
# WITH PEOPLE

"I feel like we're vibrating on the same frequency" or "I feel as though I'm on the same wavelength as you" – have you ever said or thought this about someone? We use these phrases to talk about a connection with a person that feels significant – whether it's a romantic partner or a friend/colleague with whom we feel in harmony. These are the people who understand us best, who seem to know what is going on with us without being told, and who often share our sense of humour, passions, and key motivators in life.

In Chapter 1, we talked about picking up vibes from somebody when you meet them and how this perception can influence subsequent interactions and relations with the person. This chapter is not about first impressions, it's about getting into a groove with somebody such that you feel something more is going on – as if you're "tuned in to" each other, as we say. This type of vibe can be one of the great joys in life.

In this chapter I look at what is happening when we talk about being in sync with another person, and I describe a gratitude ritual that is designed to "raise" your vibrational frequency and methods to shift your vibes to connect more deeply with a partner in a tantric sex practice. I'll start with explaining "frequency" and "wavelength" to clear up any confusion.

## *Frequency versus wavelength*

Phrases like "vibrating on the same frequency" are used to describe how people feel connections with those they are close to. Examples range from someone you might work well with – sharing similar values and priorities that mean you work well together, communicate effectively, and often succeed where others don't. On the other end of the spectrum is feeling on the same spiritual wavelength with somebody as an experience of profound interconnection.

It's interesting that the words "frequency" and "wavelength" are often used interchangeably when people are talking about being "in tune" with somebody else's vibe, but these are not technically the same. Frequency and wavelength refer to two different aspects of vibrations. The physics definition of "frequency" is the rate at which a vibration occurs, usually measured per second – as in cycles per second or Hertz. The "cycles"

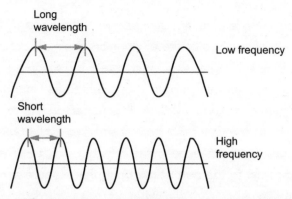

**Figure 1. Relationship between frequency and wavelength in physics.** This illustrates why, despite the physics definitions, it makes sense to use frequency and wavelength interchangeably when talking about having a similar vibe with somebody because the two terms are just two different ways to talk about vibes.

that are being counted are the waves of the vibration. The scientific definition of "wavelength" is the distance between successive crests of a wave (usually measured in meters). The faster the frequency of a vibration's wave, the shorter the wavelength (See Figure 1).

## *Brain scan shows mind meld*

Saying that you're on the same frequency as someone is a way of suggesting you have similar thought patterns, and researchers have found evidence of this by looking at brain activity. Greg Stephens and colleagues at Princeton University demonstrated that when we relate to another person telling a story the activity in our brains literally mirrors theirs (Stephens, et al., 2010). This was discovered by scanning the brains of pairs of people using functional magnetic resonance imaging (fMRI) while one person was telling a story to the other. An fMRI scan takes advantage of the fact that increased brain activity leads to greater blood flow to the part of the brain that is more active, so researchers can see what parts of the brain are "lighting up" in real time by tracking changes in blood flow. They found that brain scans of the storyteller and the listener showed their neural activity synchronizing during storytelling. It looks like the dyad was experiencing a mind meld because the same parts of the brain that lit up in the storyteller's brain would also do so in the listener's brain, after a short delay. One person is talking and recalling memories but the other is listening – so sound waves are hitting the eardrum and being translated into cognition and imagination of a novel situation (not recalling a memory) – and yet, when you look at the brain activity, you see the same patterns of activity. The technical term for this is "neural coupling." Even more remarkably, the more connected the listener said that they felt during the story, the closer the coupling of brain activity. Since this original discovery, independent labs have confirmed the importance of speaker-listening neural coupling in successful verbal communication in general (Liu, 2020). These fMRI results represent a brain wave correlate of the feeling of being "on the same wavelength" – which is super cool because when you look at the images, you're seeing a depiction of conscious vibes in action.

## Brain scans of empathy

Another conscious vibes example of feeling "on the same wavelength" is empathy – the ability to interpret the emotional states of others, and experience similar emotions. Brain-imaging studies indicate that specific brain regions show this complex emotional response to information coming into your senses from another person. One of the regions that is of particular interest in this regard is the mirror neuron system (Corradini and Antonietti, 2013). Mirror neurons were discovered by happenstance in monkeys (Gallese et al., 1996). They are special brain cells (or neurons) that respond equally when a monkey performs an action and when it witnesses another monkey perform the same action. Their fortuitous discovery occurred because monkeys' mirror neurons also respond when the monkey witnesses a person performing the same action. Researchers at the University of Parma in Italy were recording a monkey brain cell that was active when the monkey reached and picked something up, like a peanut, and were astonished to notice that the cell also activated when a researcher picked up a peanut to hand to the monkey.

So far, scientists have not been able to demonstrate that humans have individual mirror neurons like monkeys, but they have used fMRI to show that we do have a more general mirroring system because they can see groups of neurons responding equally when people perform an action and when they witness someone else perform the same action. And the types of "mirroring" that have been demonstrated in studies of the human mirror neuron system go beyond just reaction to witnessing overt actions like reaching for a peanut – the mirroring also occurs when witnessing emotions. Groups of neurons in our mirror neuron system activate when we experience an emotion and similarly when we see others experiencing an emotion. The activity in our brains is the same in both cases – so, in a sense, we are actually experiencing the emotion firsthand.

## *We are all vibrating?*

To understand how subconscious vibes come into play when people talk about having a vibration level, let's go back to the Max Plank quote from the Preface and unpack it a bit further. It is true that we – like everything – "are composed of vibration" because the human body is made up of cells, which are made up of atoms, which are made up of subatomic particles (like electrons), which are themselves just vibrating energy. So, it is also true that we are all made up of energy – vibrating energy.

The typical drawing of an atom depicts a nucleus with electrons orbiting around it. The distance across the span of electron orbits is typically more than a million times smaller than a meter and the diameter of a nucleus is 10,000–100,000 times smaller than that. This leaves a vast amount of empty space in between the subatomic particles in each atom. If all the empty space were extracted from our body's atoms, the leftover vibrating particles could be compressed to the size of a speck of dust.

The fact that our bodies are made up of mostly empty space with vibrating energy bits provides a clear scientific basis for discussing vibrating on the same frequency as someone. Since we are all vibrating energy, it is conceivable that the frequency of our vibrations could be more "in tune" with the frequency of some people more than others. Similarly, the concept of "raising your vibrational frequency" is based on the fact that our very existence is a manifestation of the vibrations within our individual inner space.

## *Vibrating on a higher frequency*

"Higher frequency vibrations" are associated with elevated emotions like happiness, joy, gratitude, and forgiveness, and with increased vitality and expanded awareness. Lower vibrations are associated with negative emotions, like anger, sadness, and pessimism. Neither of these figures of speech is meant to be taken literally. The difference between the pattern discovered in the heart EMF emanating from a person in a state of deep gratitude compared to that emanating from a person recalling feelings of anger was not actually a matter of higher or lower frequencies in the EMFs; the difference was a matter of smoothness and uniformity of the EMF pattern. Scientific measurements of actual vibrations in the human body vary greatly depending on which part of the body is being measured and at which scale (i.e. at the molecular level versus at the tissue level). Nevertheless, these figures of speech capture the essence of the relationship between our fundamental vibrational nature and our aspirations for personal growth and fulfilment. The higher your vibration is, the more in touch you are with your "higher self."

## *Raising the frequency of your vibes*

Before attempting to tune in to the same frequency as someone, it is advisable to "raise the frequency" of your own vibes. It is easy to find instructions for tuning into higher vibes in almost any book you find in the metaphysics section of a bookstore. According to esoteric knowledge passed down through numerous mystical traditions, you can raise the frequency of your vibes by eating healthy foods, reducing or eliminating alcohol and toxins from your body, thinking positive thoughts, forgiving somebody that you are holding a resentment toward, and experiencing gratitude, among other actions. I've chosen to share a vibe-raising method based on experiencing gratitude here because of the HeartMath research summarized in the previous chapter showing that experiencing deep gratitude can influence the EMF radiating from the heart.

In addition to this scientific evidence linking gratitude to EMF vibes, there is also evidence that increased gratitude helps people sleep better. Researchers from the Universities of Manchester, Nottingham and Warwick found that greater gratitude predicted better sleep quality and sleep duration (Wood, et al., 2009). They concluded that these improvements in sleep related to what was on people's minds at the end of the day. The results showed that grateful people, when falling asleep, are less likely to think negative and worrying thoughts, and are more likely to think positively.

# *Gratitude ritual*

One powerful method to experience more gratitude in your life is to include expressions of gratitude as part of your morning ritual.

1. You could begin by carrying out a simple mental gratitude exercise first thing in the morning several times a week.
2. Immediately upon waking, reflect on things for which you are grateful and say thank you for them to yourself inwardly.
3. If you prefer, tie in this regular practice to part of your morning routine, such as brushing your teeth or your hair.
4. Another version of this daily gratitude practice is to keep a gratitude journal. Both methods interweave a sustainable theme of thankfulness into your life.
5. You can also give yourself spontaneous doses of gratitude by pausing at any point in the day and turning your attention to what you are thankful for in that moment.
6. Another lovely way to get a dose of gratitude is to take a gratitude stroll. Go for a walk with the intention to find and appreciate positive things.

Further research at the University of California has shown that a grateful outlook is associated with heightened wellbeing (Emmons and McCullough, 2003). An important nuance brought out by this research is that there are two key components to practicing gratitude well for positive benefits and raised vibes:

1. We affirm the good things we've received, and
2. We acknowledge the role other people play in providing our lives with goodness.

This second component is the basis for another powerful method to experience more gratitude in your life – the gratitude letter. Think of someone who has exerted a positive influence in your life but whom you have not properly thanked and write them a letter expressing your gratitude. The letter doesn't need to be long but ensure that you're specific about what the person did and how it affected you. Building gratitude letters into your weekly or monthly schedules will sustain this outpouring of thankfulness vibes.

Researchers at the University of Pennsylvania tested the benefit of writing gratitude letters, compared to four other positive psychology interventions and to a control assignment of writing about early memories. They found that when their week's assignment was to write and personally deliver a letter of gratitude to someone who had never been properly thanked for his or her kindness, participants experienced a lasting boost in happiness levels and this impact was greater than that from the other interventions and the control assignment (Seligman, et al., 2005).

Once you have raised the frequency of your own vibes, you'll be in an optimal place for getting on the same frequency with somebody else.

## *Subtle energy connection*

Tantric sex practices can be a powerful way to become "in tune" with another person. These practices are a modern, Westernized form of tantra, which refers to ancient traditions associated with the balance of subtle energy and the interweaving of these subtle energies to create a positive outcome. It combines ideas originating from India through Hindu and Buddhist scriptures with modern sexual ideologies. Tantric sex can be thought of as a deeply spiritual form of lovemaking without the religious rituals associated with ancient forms of tantra. The practice of tantric sex is not only a physical practice, its theoretical basis focuses on connecting with your partner and yourself at the level of subtle energies vibes. The goal of tantric sex is to move "sexual energy" between you and your partner to facilitate healing, transformation and spiritual growth. I don't know of any research that has determined whether the sexual energy referred to is actually a form of subtle energy vibes or whether it is a metaphor for the physiological benefits and increased intimacy that result from the practices. There is also no research refuting this claim.

One of the most basic tantric sex teachings to cultivate sexual energy is the practice of prolonged sexual arousal and activity, without male ejaculation and with multiple female orgasms. While no studies have explicitly focused on this technique, the neurobiology of sex explains the health benefits of increased intimacy with your partner because as we spend more time sexually aroused, more beneficial hormones pump out into our bloodstream (Motofei and Rowland, 2005).

## *Human growth hormone*

The potential for increased production of human growth hormone (HGH) is a great example. This hormone – sometimes referred to as the "Fountain of Youth" hormone because it plays an important role in maintaining the health of tissues and organs – has a role in the regulation of the sexual response of genitalia. While this is potentially the case for women (Galdiero, et al., 2012), most of the research in this area has focused on the link between HGH and the swelling of the erectile tissue of the penis due to engorgement with blood.

Researchers at Hannover Medical School in Germany discovered some of the first evidence of this connection by measuring the levels of HGH in the circulating blood of 35 healthy potent volunteers during different conditions of the penis, including flaccidity, tumescence, rigidity and detumescence (Becker, et al., 2000). They found the main increase in HGH was during the development of penile tumescence. Subsequent experiments by the same group corroborated this finding and allowed this group to conclude that HGH may be of major importance in the maintenance of male erectile capability through the stimulation of signaling pathways in the cells of the spongy tissue that runs through the shaft of the penis (Becker, et al., 2002). With that information, it seems likely that extending the period of readiness for sexual activity could result in increased levels of this beneficial hormone in your bloodstream.

## *Oxytocin*

With regard to intimacy, the "cuddle hormone" oxytocin also has an important connection with sexual arousal. Oxytocin was originally discovered as a bonding hormone because of its role in sealing a selective and lasting bond between mother and offspring. To explain briefly, your hypothalamus makes oxytocin, but it is stored and released into your bloodstream on certain signals, such as in response to various emotional social situations (e.g., parent-infant contact) and when sensory neurons are stimulated (e.g., stimulation of the nipples) and low intensity stimulation of the skin, e.g., in response to touch and stroking.

For humans and other mammals, simply the presence of an infant causes the release of oxytocin in adults (Feldman, 2012; Kenkle, et al., 2012). This hormone triggers feelings of love and protection, so babies are basically able to chemically manipulate us into loving and caring for them when young and vulnerable. The dynamic is comparable to the chemical triggering of subconscious vibes described earlier relating to sweat and tears, except that in this case, the trigger hormone is produced inside the same person on whom it has the effect.

Oxytocin got it nickname as the "cuddle hormone" because its effect of triggering feelings of love and protection is not limited to parent and offspring – it works between lovers as well. Anthropologist Helen Fisher has shown with brain scans that merely viewing a photograph of one's beloved unleashes a flood of neurochemicals – testosterone, oxytocin, dopamine, norepinephrine – that amp up feelings of tenderness and attraction (Fisher, et al., 2005).

There are no studies specifically measuring oxytocin during tantric sex but a recent systematic review evaluating 13 studies measuring oxytocin levels during the induction of sexual arousal and orgasm found consistent increases in both women and men (Cera, et al., 2021). This is good news for tantric sex partners because more oxytocin is pumped into your bloodstream when you are sexually aroused, and since sexual arousal and orgasm increase hormone levels, prolonging those activities will lead to further increases that could then trigger even stronger feelings of love and protection with your partner.

Tantric teachings also emphasize slow breathing and mindful touching. The idea is to be fully in the present moment and absorb every feeling and sensation. Another advantage of tantric sex is a release from expectations, such as the expectation that penetration will occur, and concerns around whether you or your partner will reach climax. Letting go of these expectations is one way that tantric sex encourages lovers to relax and enjoy the present moment, promoting a deeper spiritual awareness around the sexual experience, and a deeper connection with your partner. Through breathing, massage or prolonged eye contact, you can promote the feeling of vibrating on the same frequency for a more intimate experience.

## *Tips for tantric sex*

There are plenty of resources for learning about tantric sex, including the Institute for Authentic Tantra Education (authentictantra.com) and the book *Urban Tantra,* by acclaimed sex educator Barbara Carrellas, which teaches more than one hundred easy-to-follow techniques and is inclusive of trans and gender nonconforming people (Carrellas and Sprinkle, 2007). Here are a few general first steps to give you a taste of tantra:

1. Prepare a safe space. Creating a safe space is an important step and, if the idea resonates with you, think of it as creating a sacred space. Choose bedding that feels luxurious and invest in high-quality candles, clean the room and remove all clutter, and adjust the lighting and soundscape as you prefer.
2. Prepare yourself. Take a bath or shower and put on clothing that makes you feel relaxed and sensual. Turn off your phone and do a short meditation to quiet your mind.
3. Begin with "eye gazing." Face your partner and look into each other's eyes. This may feel uncomfortable at first so go ahead and let the giggles out. After a while, you will relax and begin to feel an energetic connection with

your partner. It may actually feel like vibrations. Hold hands during this step or synchronize your breathing to help tune in to each other.

4. Tantric massage. A great next step is tantric massage. Decide who will be giving the massage and who will be receiving first. These roles are switched mid-way. The Receiver's job is to relax and accept any and all pleasurable vibes coming their way. The partner giving the massage focuses on giving them pleasure. Allow your thoughts to cease and just feel. Try to tune in to what your partner's body is calling out for.

5. Edging is bringing your partner to the brink of climax in cycles. You get to the point of orgasm and then stop stimulation, wait and then start the build-up all over again. Some people find that this technique makes their orgasm more intense, once it does occur.

I've included this introduction to tantric sex in this chapter because it is an effective way to the feeling of vibrating on the same frequency as someone. Similar to the slow-breathing technique in Chapter 1, tantric sex helps to turn on your biophysical vibes and is a "no-brainer" method to turn off your thinking and worrying mind.

As with all other types of meditation, if you notice that your attention has drifted away from the present, you're thinking about the future or the past, just acknowledge that and, without judging yourself, return to the present. Perhaps the biggest advantage of tantric sex is that you get the benefits of meditation – quiet mind and all that jazz – plus you may get to deepen your connection with your partner.

## SUMMARY

- Feeling as if you're "on the same wavelength" happens when you have experiences with a person where you find yourself feeling that you have similar outlooks on life or even similar ways of working; it also includes experiences of deep interconnection.
- Frequency and wavelength are not the same thing – they're different aspects of the cycle of a vibration; long wavelengths lead to low frequency and short wavelengths to high frequency.
- Brain scans have shown that there may be a biophysical basis for the feeling that you're

"on the same wavelength" as someone: "neural coupling" is when recounting stories connects storytellers and listeners as the listener's brain activity will mimic that of the person telling the story.

- Remember that our bodies are made up mostly of empty space filled with vibrating energy – a clear basis for the idea of being on the same frequency or wavelength as other people.

- Several hormones are linked to close physical contact with those we care about – HGH as part of sexual arousal and oxytocin as the hormone that bonds a carer to a baby – invoking vibes that will protect and support the baby in its infancy.

- Similarly, simply looking at a picture of a beloved partner unleashes numerous chemicals, including testosterone, oxytocin, dopamine and norepinephrine.

- There are some very simple and positive ways to raise the frequency of your vibes and deepen your connection with others using gratitude methods and tantric sex.

# CHAPTER 3

---

# PSYCHIC CONNECTION WITH A LOVED ONE IN DISTRESS

Returning home late from a high school dance, I crept into my house in stealth mode, hoping that my parents would already be asleep. No such luck. My dad was still up, and he looked agitated. He called me into the kitchen with a line of questioning at the ready. Thankfully, the atmosphere mellowed as soon as he was sure that I was alright. He told me that he'd had a weird feeling while I was at the dance, as if I was in danger somehow. This was before cell phones, so he'd just fretted until I got home. I was stunned because it seemed as if he had read my mind from a distance. I had indeed felt in danger, terrified even, at the dance, because I had been told that Miles Furnish was going to beat me up – because I had asked Kirsten Finstad to dance. I didn't know how to fight and Miles was a big, buff guy so an injury seemed imminent. It didn't happen, thankfully, but it had made for a tense evening.

It made a certain amount of sense to me that my mind would have either intentionally sent out distress signals on the psychic airwaves, or unintentionally leaked them out. Of course, my dad's acute bout of worrying about me could have just been a coincidence. It didn't feel like it though, for a couple of reasons. Firstly, my dad had never told me that he was worried about me when I was out before. Secondly, I had never before come anywhere near as close to being physically assaulted as I had that night.

I believe that my dad's timely worrying was more than just a coincidence, and I am not alone in believing that psychic distress calls can be picked up by loved ones. In this chapter, we'll consider how subconscious vibes could be enabling these psychic connections in times of distress. We'll also review some of the relevant science and discuss a simple practical technique that is an evidence-based method to reduce worrying and anxiety.

## *"Can your sixth sense tell when a loved one has died miles away?"*

This was the headline of a story in the newspaper in December 2011. The journalist recounted the story of Annie Cap, who firmly believes she received a psychic distress call from her mother from across the globe at the exact time that her mother began suffocating in her hospital bed. Annie was living in London, England, at the time and had known that her mother was in the hospital near their family home on the west coast of the United States. Her sister was with their mom and had assured Annie that the hospital visit was nothing to worry about. She said that there appeared to be nothing wrong with their mother but that she had fainted, so the doctors wanted to keep her overnight to run a few routine tests. Everybody expected that she would be out of the hospital the next day. Even with these assurances, it would be natural for Annie to feel a bit worried but what she experienced was much more significant than worrying. It was more like a panic attack. She was at work and suddenly found herself struggling to breathe for no apparent reason. One minute everything was normal and the next she was clutching at her chest and gasping for air. She recounts in her book, titled *Beyond Goodbye* (Cap, 2011): ". . . I began uncontrollably gagging and coughing. I could hardly breathe and I felt like I was drowning or suffocating. It came on without warning, from out of nowhere, so extreme and intense. I was wheezing and had a strange gurgling cough. Nothing I did seemed to stop it fully."

Amid her panic, she felt compelled to call the hospital to check on her mother. Her sister answered the phone in their mother's room and was in a panic herself because their mother had just moments earlier taken a turn for the worse. She quickly explained that their mother was having long gaps between labored breaths – she was drowning in her own fluids, because her heart was no longer beating strongly enough to keep the fluid from accumulating in her lungs. Annie could hear her mother making the same strange gurgling cough that she had experienced just minutes earlier. Annie's sister was able to hold the telephone handset up to their mother's ear in time for her to say, "I love you, Mom," over and over as their mother took her last breath and passed away.

Annie believes that her mother was reaching out across the psychic airwaves to her to say goodbye and what happened was an empathic death experience, in which she physically felt her mother's fatal symptoms.

## *How do psychic "airwaves" work?*

How could Annie Cap sense her mother's desire to connect with her as she was dying? What happened on the night that I asked Kirsten Finstad to dance that allowed my dad to sense my fear? What about other stories we've all heard about people calling loved ones when they are struggling or knowing when close relations are in trouble?

I believe that picking up "psychic vibes" is an instance of "tuning in" to close family members, as well as unrelated but "bonded" people, by way of a spike in the subconscious information channels that exist as part of the deep interconnectedness between people. In other words, there are no "airwaves" needed because our minds are already connected at the subconscious level and urgent situations can bring information to the surface as vibes.

To map out my hypothesis about how this could happen, and regarding how my dad got the memo about me paralyzed with fright at the dance, think of me as Person A in the figure below and my dad as Person B. This depiction of how two people's minds overlap is adapted from ideas from psychology and quantum

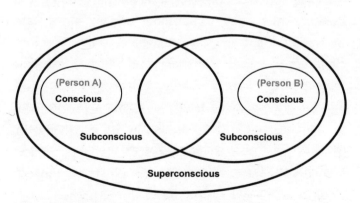

**Figure 2. Theoretical model of overlap between two people's minds**

physics (Brabant, 2016). Firstly, I want to draw your attention to the fact that the only part of Person A's mind that is completely separate from Person B's mind is the little bubble representing the conscious mind. The concept that there are aspects of the subconscious mind shared between all people is attributed to Carl Jung, who – along with Sigmund Freud – is considered one of the founders of modern psychotherapy (Mayer, 2002). Jung's idea of a "collective unconscious" is based on humanity's shared experiences.

Lastly, the largest bubble labeled "Superconscious" represents the "interconnected with everything mind," sometimes referred to as the higher self. The famous English poet Alfred, Lord Tennyson is quoted as saying that superconsciousness is a state where "individuality itself seemed to dissolve and fade away into boundless being," which was "no nebulous ecstasy, but a state of transcendent wonder, associated with absolute clearness of mind" (Yogananda, 1994). I've included the superconscious bubble here because this level of mind is often invoked to explain psychic phenomena in general, but I don't think that it is necessarily required for the "psychic" vibes we're considering in this chapter. (We will get to superconscious vibes in Chapters 7 and 8.)

To consider psychic vibes between loved ones, imagine emotions and thoughts radiating out from

Person A like the path of a skipping stone across a pond, from the conscious and into the subconscious mind. Normally, the stone sinks after two or three touches in the shallow part of the subconscious but imagine we are mapping the night of the dangerous dance with Kirsten Finstad. When the information pertains to a perceived threatening or otherwise highly charged situation, it reverberates through to the deeper subconscious mind and can reach the place of overlap with Person B's subconscious mind – see Figure 3 below.

The final skip of the stone into Person B's little conscious mind bubble represents the information "bubbling up" to Person B's awareness as a subconscious vibe. Note that a subconscious vibe

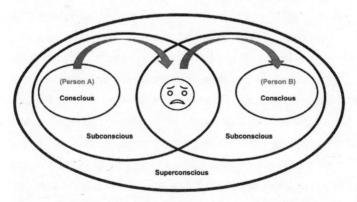

**Figure 3. Theoretical path of subconscious vibes between two people.**

doesn't turn into a conscious vibe when this happens, but some awareness reaches the conscious mind. The information can get a little blurry as it skips across the pond due to crossing multiple mind level boundaries. With my dad, it became a vague feeling that I was in trouble, and in Annie Cap's case it manifested as her sharing similar physical sensations to her mother plus the compulsion to reach out and call her.

## *Easing your thoughts when worried*

Psychic distress calls are rare but what is not uncommon for many of us is a preoccupation with problems that we don't even have, the ongoing pondering of worst-case scenarios and constantly prepping ourselves for dire happenings. As mentioned earlier, keeping our vibrations as positive as possible is beneficial to us in many ways, so I want to share a simple but powerful technique and great antidote for worrying and anxiety called Emotional Freedom Technique (EFT). EFT is a popular form of biofield therapy that combines acupressure – to stimulate the body's subtle energies – with elements of established psychotherapy methods like cognitive behavioral therapy, which is an evidence-based talk therapy that challenges negative patterns of thought about the self and the world in order to alter unwanted behavior patterns.

EFT is often referred to as "tapping," because the acupressure is self-administered by tapping certain spots on the body. Similar to acupuncture (the Traditional Chinese Medicine practice of the insertion of fine needles into the body at key energy points), EFT focuses on the TCM meridian points – or qi nexus hot spots – and is thought to restore balance to your body's subtle energy system. Whereas acupuncture uses needles to stimulate qi flow through these points, acupressure and EFT use fingers.

One of the things that EFT seems to do is rewire your brain so that stress loops get ironed out (more on this below). Returning to the parent-child theme, I used EFT when I found myself fretting about my daughter's safety for no good reason. She was on her first road trip with her friends. They were driving to Lake Tahoe and there was a winter storm in the forecast. Before she headed out, we had already done everything that I could think of to be sure that they would be safe. Off they went and up went my anxiety. I realized that the best thing for me to do was to let go of the fear that wasn't doing anybody any good. I was able to accomplish this by spending about ten minutes practicing the EFT method described below.

# *EFT tapping instructions*

EFT is easy to learn, and you can practice it almost anywhere. I'll share a version of the steps to follow, and you can refer to Figure 4 on page 63 as you review the steps. Keep in mind that the statements to say to yourself are not set in stone – feel free to alter them as you wish to best convey the same meaning, and don't worry if you accidentally switch some words around.

1. Identify the fear that you want to let go of and check in with yourself to see where you are starting, in terms of anxiety level. Give a score to how much stress you are feeling right now on a scale of 0–10, with 10 being the worst or most difficult. Close your eyes and take a gentle breath in and out, slowly. Now take another gentle breath and, this time, pay attention to how deep your breath is. Is it full and going down deep into your belly, relaxed and open? Or is it tight and constricted and high up in your chest? As you continue to pay attention to your breath, tune in to any anxiety that you might be feeling.

2. Now begin the tapping. With your eyes open or closed, start off by tapping on your non-dominant hand at the point that is nicknamed the **karate chop point**. It is below the little finger on the outside edge of the hand. Tap with four fingers of

your dominant hand, held loosely, on the karate chop point of the other hand.

3. While tapping gently, state aloud or inside your head several times: *"Even though I feel so much anxiety about everything that's going on, I deeply and completely accept myself."* Repeat again with similar language, for example: *"Even though this feels so overwhelming, I choose to relax and feel safe now."* And then make a third statement while still tapping, something like: *"Even though I'm feeling so much anxiety, it's safe to let it go now."* You can just stick with this one point, if you like, and skip to step #13.

4. If you choose to move on to other points, switch to tapping the karate chop point on the other hand, repeating the statements in #3, and then move on to the face points.

5. The first face point is **the center of the eyebrows**, just above the nose. Use two fingers of one hand (or both hands at the same time). Tapping and breathing gently, while tuning into the anxiety, the goal is to counteract the feelings with the calming signals to the brain from the tapping.

6. When you're ready, move to the second face point, at the very **edge of the eyebrows** (where you can feel the bone of your eye socket). You can tap both sides, or just one. Take a moment to

think about just how overwhelmed you are while you are tapping here. There is so much going on, and that is okay.

7. When you feel ready, move to the third face point, **underneath the center of each eye** – either on one side or under both eyes together. Again, you know you're tapping on the right spot when you can feel the bone. Don't worry about getting it perfect. Take a moment to think about just how overwhelmed you are. Say to yourself something like: *"It is safe to feel this anxiety,"* while continuing to tap.

8. The fourth face point is under the nose, **just above the upper lip**. Say to yourself something like: *"And it is safe to begin to let the anxiety go."*

9. The fifth face point is **beneath the lower lip**, above the chin. Tap with two fingers in that little crease, saying: *"It is safe to feel this anxiety."*

10. The next point is **just below the collar bones**. Feel for the bone on each side, just below where the neck joins the chest, and tap about an inch below that. You can use all ten fingers on this point. Say to yourself something like: *"It is safe to feel this anxiety."*

11. The next point is on the side of the torso, about three inches **below the armpits** on either side

of the body. Tap, saying: "It is safe to feel all
this stress."

12. The last point is at the **top of the head** (the
crown chakra). Tap there and say: "And it is safe
to let it go."

13. End with a deep, slow breath in and out. That
was one round of tapping.

14. Repeat the sequence as many times as you like
and alter the affirmations as you wish as you go.

15. To finish, assess your anxiety level and give a new
score. Hopefully, the score has decreased. If it

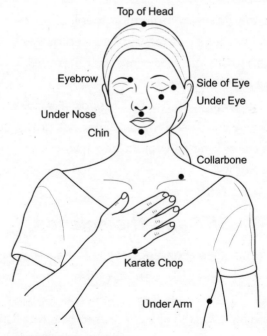

**Figure 4. EFT Tapping Points**

hasn't, or hasn't decreased as much as you would like it to, repeat the rounds of tapping until it does.

Sometimes we start tapping because we want to deal with anxiety about one topic and then, after a round of tapping and checking in, it occurs to us that it is actually a different topic causing the anxiety. In this case, start another round of tapping focusing on the new topic. The formula for coming up with your positive statement is to identify a problem and make a statement about accepting yourself despite the problem. A common template is: "Even though I have this [fear or problem], I deeply and completely accept myself." For example, I started out with, "Even though I'm anxious about my daughter driving on the highway in snowy conditions, I deeply and completely accept myself." After a few rounds, I switched it to "Even though I'm sad my daughter has grown up and doesn't need me to protect her anymore, it's safe to let it go now."

## *EFT and the science*

More than one hundred clinical trials have been conducted on EFT and together they make a compelling case that it is a safe, "evidence-based" practice for reducing anxiety caused by stress (Church, et al., 2018a). One of the leading theories for how EFT works, the Amygdala Desensitization and Counter-Conditioning Theory, is based on the idea that the subtle vibrations stimulated by tapping on the body's acupressure points rewire the connections to the part of the brain that is in charge of detecting threats – the amygdala (Lane, 2009). It is already known that negative emotions are perceived as a threat by the amygdala, in much the same way as a real physical threat would be. The amygdala is part of the midbrain, or limbic system, where emotional memories are encoded, and it works with other brain regions (e.g., the hippocampus) to generate primary emotions from external perceptions and internal thoughts. In other words, it helps to emotionally charge and label our experiences for our brains to file away and then to warn us about situations that we might encounter in the future. The genius of EFT is in its combination of activating this emotion-reaction circuit with acupressure (tapping) while self-administering hypnotic suggestions to feel calm. Stimulating the subtle energy pathways by tapping the appropriate acupressure points while performing self-hypnosis rewires the brain so that external perceptions that had previously triggered fear are uncoupled from scary internal thoughts, allowing us to experience a calming peacefulness.

Our team at IONS conducted the first randomized controlled trial of EFT, measuring a physiological biomarker of stress before and after treatment. In collaboration with Dawson Church, a luminary in the field, we measured cortisol levels in healthy volunteers before and after a single session of EFT and found positive effects (Church, et al., 2012). In our study, 83 participants were randomly assigned to a one-time hour-long session of three different experimental conditions: EFT, talk therapy in the form of a supportive interview, and rest. Cortisol, a hormone associated with high stress levels, was measured before and after the treatments. The results showed a significantly lower level of cortisol in the EFT group (24%) compared to the two other therapy groups, which showed a decline of only an average of 14%. The reduction in this primary stress hormone was also positively associated with a reduction in a range of psychological symptoms, including anxiety and depression.

## *EFT and your genes*

Given the wide-ranging clinical benefits reported for EFT, it is likely that genomic mechanisms play a role in its effects on the body. We conducted an exploratory study to get an idea if we could see evidence of this.

In our study, sixteen veterans with PTSD symptoms participated in a 10-week intervention of treatment sessions plus learning to use tapping at home. We found that the intervention was very effective in reducing PTSD symptoms in the EFT group, compared to the control group. Moreover, the veterans maintained their improvements when assessed at a 6-month follow-up. When we compared genomic data before and after, we identified six genes (Church, et al., 2018b) and two noncoding in-between bits (Yount, et al., 2019) that correlated with successful PTSD treatment.

I share this science that's been done regarding EFT to encourage you to give it a try. If you do and it feels like tapping is working for you, why not advance your practice by following a video online (e.g., "Nick Ortner's Tapping Technique to Calm Anxiety and Stress in 3 minutes") or finding a professional to guide you through EFT therapy sessions. I recommend choosing somebody certified in "Clinical EFT" as this is the standardized method for therapeutic sessions used in most of the published clinical trials.

# SUMMARY

- "Psychic" vibes with loved ones in distress may be possible due to information channels that exist as part of interconnected subconscious minds.
- Modern psychology and quantum physics support a theoretical model of mind that allows for deep interconnectedness between people.
- Research has shown EFT as a simple and effective antidote for worrying and anxiety that takes advantage of the techniques developed through TCM (acupressure) and hypnotherapy/CBT. One of the leading theories as to how it works involves subtle vibrations stimulated by tapping on acupressure points alongside self-hypnosis.
- EFT was shown to significantly reduce levels of the stress hormone cortisol in a controlled trial compared to other treatments.

# CHAPTER 4

## ARE YOU BEING STARED AT?

We've looked at times of distress and how they might generate subconscious vibes felt from a distance. Now we'll shift to a seemingly more straight-forward topic – the sensation of being stared at from behind – which has been explored in some fascinating scientific research.

I'll start with the landmark publication that kicked off the scientific debate over the feeling of being stared at more than 100 years ago: Professor E.B. Titchener wrote about his first-year students at a prestigious university:

*"Every year I find a certain proportion of students . . . who are firmly persuaded that they can 'feel' that they are being stared at from behind, and a smaller proportion who believe that, by persistent gazing at the back of the neck, they have the power of making a person seated in front of them turn around and look them in the face." (Titchener, 1898)*

Shortly after, in 1913, a survey of Stanford University students found that two-thirds of them believed in this phenomenon (Coover, 1913). More recent surveys in both Europe and North America have found that between 70% and 97% of the people questioned said they had had personal experiences of this occurrence (Sheldrake, 2005). Research on this topic continues today and this chapter will include an abbreviated tour of what has been uncovered, plus a couple of fascinating instances of related studies exploring whether cells in Petri dishes or our "gut brains" can pick up vibes sent from a distance.

I've chosen a practical application to share that involves directing good vibes toward other people – rather than just staring at them. It is called Loving-Kindness Meditation and I recommend it as a fool-proof method to strengthen feelings of connection toward others and, again, to raise your own vibrations to a higher level.

## *Scopaesthesia*

Professor E. B. Titchener's report quoted on page 69 was published in a scientific journal that was, and still is, one of the "holy grails" of journals for scientists. Titchener's take on the phenomenon – the scientific term being "scopaesthesia" (which is pronounced "scope-as-thee-sia") – was that it is just a trick of the mind and there is no need to invoke any ideas about "vibes" to explain it.

Titchener's students described this feeling of scopaesthesia as a state of unpleasant tingling, which gathers in volume and intensity until a movement that shall relieve it becomes inevitable. The movement referred to is when you turn to check whether someone is staring at you. Titchener's theory was that people normally get nervous about guarding their back and therefore experience a build-up of nervous energy when seated in front of others, say in a lecture hall. When they turn to check, the turning motion draws the gaze of somebody behind them. It takes longer for the person in front to turn their head than for the person in the rear to shift the direction of their eyes. The result is that the person in front sees the gaze locked on them and can mistakenly assume it is the cause of their tingly feeling. Without describing the details of the experiments, Titchener reported that he had tested scopaesthesia:

*"in a series of laboratory experiments conducted with persons who declared themselves either peculiarly susceptible to the stare or peculiarly capable of making people turn round. As regards such capacity and susceptibility, the experiments have invariably given a negative result."*

Later studies of scopaesthesia produced both negative and positive results. The negative camp included research from John E. Coover, who reported in 1913 that over half of his students at Stanford University believed they could sometimes feel when somebody was staring at them from behind but failed to do so under experimental conditions (Coover, 1913).

Another notable naysayer was Isabelle Mareschal at the University of Sydney, who reported negative results of scopaesthesia experiments conducted with her colleagues in 2013 (Mareschal, et al., 2013). This group argued that humans are hard-wired to feel people are staring at us, even when they aren't. They suggested this hard-wiring is a kind of safeguard designed to make us ready for interaction just in case something actually happens.

However, positive study results started to roll in after scientists adopted a different strategy for testing scopaesthesia. Instead of relying on people to say or write down whether they felt like somebody was staring at them, Marilyn Schlitz and Stephen LaBerge measured it by looking for subconscious reactions, by monitoring electrodermal activity, which is a measure of the electrical activity of our skin (Schlitz and LaBerge, 1997). Getting scientific about it, electrodermal activity is a measure of the levels of electrical *resistance* of the skin to a small electrical current, the skin's electrical resistance largely being determined by the sweat glands.

## *Here we go with sweat again . . .*

Not to be confused with the armpit sweat research discussed earlier, electrodermal activity is usually detected by placing electrical sensors on the fingers. Yes, our fingers sweat. Even when we are not exercising or overheating, the skin all over our bodies produces tiny micro-doses of sweat that we largely don't even notice. This type of sweating is controlled by the sympathetic nervous system – remember that this branch of the autonomic nervous system is the one that runs the "fight or flight" program. When stressful situations activate the sympathetic nervous system, we sweat. This fact that sympathetic nervous system activity increases when people are stressed or feel threatened was not lost on the famous Carl Jung, and psychologists after him, who have been using electrodermal activity to study subconscious emotions in all kinds of psychology experiments since the early 1900s.

The success of applying the electrodermal activity technique to study scopaesthesia relies on whether this perception is a form of threat detection. If yes, then the sympathetic nervous system might be able to pick up such a signal subconsciously, leading to increased sweating and resulting changes in the electrodermal activity. Schlitz and others were able to gain evidence that people could tell when someone was staring at them subconsciously using this method. Then, others used the same method but got negative results (Wiseman and Smith, 1994). This discrepancy inspired the two "sides" to conduct an extended collaborative program of skeptic-proponent research (Schlitz, et al., 2006). They initially found evidence of an "experimenter effect," that is, experiments conducted by the proponent obtained significant results but those conducted by the skeptic did not. The implication seemed to be that the beliefs of the experimenters were influencing the outcomes. In other words, if the experimenter did not believe in scopaesthesia, then they might somehow influence the people being studied to suppress any staring detection ability that they might have. And, conversely, experimenters who were believers might somehow influence the research participants to allow their scopaesthesia to shine.

## *"Unknown to science"*

The biochemist Rupert Sheldrake is the most prominent proponent of scopaesthesia today. He has devised a very simple experimental protocol for testing it in which lookers and guessers work in pairs, with lookers sitting behind the guessers in a randomized sequence of trials. The lookers either look at the back of the guesser or look away and think of something else. The guesser then indicates whether they think they're being stared at. Sheldrake has found that the guessers are right more often than not, even when they were blind-folded and given no feedback. Experiments that added the condition that guessers were stared at through closed windows, so that any potential scent cues were ruled out, also found a significant excess of correct over incorrect guesses. The statistical analysis for this study produced an impressive p-value of $p < 0.004$ (Sheldrake, 2000). Typically, scientists want the p-value to be at or below 0.05 to call a result "significant." In non-statistics terms, if everything going on in the experiment was just due to chance, then you could expect to see the results that showed up in 5 out of 100 experiments. For the Sheldrake experiments, with the guessers correctly guessing when somebody was staring at them through a closed window, there's only a 0.04% chance that the guessers just got lucky. In other words, you could expect to see the results achieved only 4 times if you ran the experiment 1,000 times.

This provocative finding supporting the reality of scopaesthesia prompted Sheldrake to ask independent researchers in Canada, Germany and the United States to replicate the same experiments and they found even more significant positive effects (p < 0.0002). This series of studies has led Sheldrake to conclude that scopaesthesia is real and it originates with an influence at present unknown to science. My take on scopaesthesia is that it is likely another instance of information "bubbling up" as a subconscious vibe through the interconnectedness of subconscious minds (see figure on page 57).

## *Can plants sense if they're being stared at?*

The electrodermal activity measurements described above are sensitive to changes in the internal emotionality of an individual, one of the key components of a lie detector test (other components usually including pulse and breath rate). The lie detector test is called a polygraph test because it measures multiple ("poly") signals and scribbles them out on a single strip of moving paper ("graph"). Cleve Backster founded the United States Central Intelligence Agency's polygraph unit in the 1940s and later created the Baxter School of Lie Detection in San Diego where police officers were trained to administer the polygraph test. In the 1960s, Baxter decided to hook electrodermal activity sensors up to plant leaves to see what happened. His findings caused a sensation and were written about in the book *The Secret Life of Plants* (Tompkins and Bird, 1989). He reported that plants could react not only when they were harmed, but also when a person just threatened to harm them – as if they could sense the emotions of people. He also reported that one of his plants really didn't like the mail carrier.

## *Staring at cells in a Petri dish*

A group of scientists from the California Pacific Medical Center in San Francisco showed up to Cleve Baxter's lab to try a new kind of experiment. They were interested to see if the fascinating results he was seeing with his polygraph technique would translate into the medical realm. The mission was to see if human brain tumor cells in a Petri dish could be hooked up to Baxter's machine and if they would react, similar to the same way that plants did. If plant "consciousness" could be revealed with Baxter's machine, the "consciousness" of individual cancer cells might also. The plan was to have a psychic try to connect with cells while they were hooked up to the machine. I was fortunate to be included in the group because of my work as a biologist exploring consciousness-based phenomena plus my expertise in handling human brain tumor cells. My assignment for this mission was simply to prepare the cells and help Baxter hook them up to his polygraph machine but the plan quickly took a detour.

Baxter was chatting with me while I was using test tubes and a tabletop centrifuge to prepare the cells for the experiment. He asked me what kind of cells they were and how I kept them alive in a Petri dish. I explained that the cells originally came from a brain tumor, and they kept growing and growing because that is what cancer cells do. To keep them alive outside the body, I had to feed them regularly with a nutrient liquid and thin them out when they multiplied and got too crowded in the Petri dish. When he learned that I had been taking care of these cells for years as part of my day job studying anticancer agents, he announced a change of plan. He was certain that these cells thought of me as their daddy and that our best chance of seeing them react to somebody's attention was for me to be the person trying to connect with them. "Forget about the psychic," he said.

So, out of nowhere, I found myself standing in front of a dish of cells with wires stuck in it while the rest of the group was across the room hovering over the strip of moving paper being spat out of Baxter's polygraph machine. After checking that the little needle that scratches out a line on the paper in accordance with changes in the electrical properties picked up by the wires was working properly, they confirmed that everything looked good. The needle was drawing a straight line on the moving paper, indicating that the electrical signal from the wires was stable and they gave me the signal to "go."

I had not prepared for this duty, so I did whatever came to mind. I closed my eyes and did a short meditation to quiet my mind. After about a minute, I felt calm and centered. With my eyes closed, I said a silent prayer to the deceased person that the cells came from. I acknowledged this donor, offering respect and love, and asked for their help in revealing information that would help elevate human consciousness. Then I imagined sending out love vibes flowing from my heart to the cells for a minute or so.

When I opened my eyes and looked over at the group, they looked stunned. I walked over to look at the paper read out from the polygraph and felt even more shaken than them. The straight line being drawn by the little needle in the polygraph had changed dramatically during the few minutes that I had attempted to connect with the cells. The needle had begun zigzagging up and down so erratically that the trace reminded me of images I had seen on TV of seismograph recordings during an earthquake. I had hoped that we might see the line show some squiggles indicating that the cells were reacting to the attention but this was way beyond that.

This experience left a deep impression on me. I cannot offer it as definitive proof that the isolated cells have consciousness and we had captured evidence of them responding to attention because we had not set up rigorous experimental procedures, such as blinding and randomization. On the other hand, it was a very simple set-up and the result seemed clear cut. Baxter's polygraph showed that the electrical activity measured from the cells was stable before and after I started trying to connect with them and then went bonkers when I did. When I had stopped and walked away from the cells, the needle settled down and began tracing a straight line again. Baxter left the polygraph machine running for about 20 minutes while I recovered and the line stayed stable and straight the whole time. Something had happened during those key couple of minutes.

I believe that we witnessed evidence that at least supports the idea that individual cells do have some form of rudimentary consciousness and this enables them to react to vibes generated by our minds. Another possibility is that the cells were affected by a change in my body's EMFs when I began meditating and praying. If either of these possibilities are indeed the case, then the type of vibes we send out don't just affect others, they could be having an impact on our own health at the cellular level – all the more reason to try to send out positive vibes as much as possible.

## *Gut feeling experiment*

One possible reason that the brain tumor cells may have responded so strongly to the vibes I was putting out is that their level of consciousness is rudimentary. Their "raw" reaction was easy to pick up because they don't have a busy conscious mind like we do that could interfere by clouding the signal with internal chatter.

I want to share one more scopaesthesia-type experiment that also aimed to circumvent conscious mind interference and look for ways in which to measure a basic response in the body. IONS Scientists Marilyn Schlitz and Dean Radin hypothesized that the enteric nervous system might be good at reacting to vibes because, like the isolated cells in the Petri dishes, it is not yoked with the incessant internal chatter of our conscious mind. As mentioned in Chapter 1, the enteric nervous system (or "gut brain") is a branch of the autonomic nervous system, which controls the automatic processes of your body without us thinking about them. The gut brain is mainly in charge of digestion. While the gut brain can function independently of neural inputs from the central nervous system (the brain and spinal cord), bidirectional communication between our two brains – the gut-brain axis – is extensive and plays a role in the emergence of complex behaviors (Fleming, et al., 2020), possibly including intuitive experiences and decision making (Gershon and Margolis, 2021).

Schlitz and Radin set up an experiment to observe if the gut brain of an individual would respond to the vibes sent from a distant person (Radin and Schlitz, 2005). They recruited participants for the experiment in pairs so that one could take the role of Sender (the one attempting to send vibes) and the other the role of Receiver (the one receiving the vibes). The Receiver was asked to relax in a reclining chair inside an electromagnetically shielded room with sensors placed on their stomach to measure the electrical activity of their gut brain. (This measurement method is called electrogastrography, or EGG.) A video camera was focused on the Receiver's face and they were asked to attempt to maintain a "mental connection" with the Sender. The Receiver knew that their partner would be staring at them periodically over closed-circuit video, but did not know the timing, length or frequency.

Meanwhile in a distant room, the Sender sat in front of two video screens. One screen periodically displayed the Receiver's live image; the other displayed a sequence of pictures selected for invoking emotional responses. Music accompanied the pictures as well. The Sender was instructed to periodically stare at the Receiver with intention to send vibes to the Receiver with the emotions evoked by the pictures. Positive emotion pictures included photos of smiling babies and kittens, accompanied by the Beatles' rendition of *Twist and Shout* and by Little Richard's song, *Long Tall Sally*. Negative emotion pictures included a sad theme with pictures such as a graveyard, accompanied by Samuel Barber's *Adagio for Strings*, and an angry theme with pictures such as an atomic bomb explosion, accompanied by the song *Feuer Frei*, by the heavy metal rock band Rammstein. There were also neutral pictures to serve as a control, such as gray-hued rectangles accompanied by pink noise. To encourage a shared state of connection, the participants were asked to exchange a personal, meaningful item, like a watch or ring, and hold the items in their hands throughout the experiment.

The experiment worked. EGG values were significantly larger on average when the Sender was sending vibes while experiencing positive and negative emotions, as compared to neutral emotions. The p-values for these effects were $p = 0.006$ and $p = 0.0009$, respectively – remember that $p = 0.05$ is typically considered a threshold for calling something significant and smaller p-values are considered even more significant. So, these results are a strong indication that the gut brain can receive vibes sent by a distant person.

## *Loving-Kindness Meditation*

What kind of vibes are you sending out to people most of the time? The experiments we've reviewed in this chapter indicate that it really matters, and that we are sending out vibes just by looking at another person, which can be detected at some level, perhaps at the subconscious level (e.g., by the gut brain) or perhaps even at the level of the individual cells in our bodies. Knowing this, don't you want to be sending out good vibes and don't you want to be bathing your own cells in good vibes?

The Loving-Kindness Meditation is a tried-and-true practice for generating good vibes for yourself and for others. It focuses on expressing respect and compassion for yourself, for others, and ultimately, all living things. Considering the evidence suggesting that we can affect people and plants with our vibes, practicing intentional well-wishing toward others likely has tangible positive effects. Jon Kabat-Zinn, an internationally known scientist and meditation teacher, describes Loving-Kindness Meditation as a "heartscape meditation" for deep healing of ourselves and others. There are many variations of this practice. Here's a version that I've adapted from watching online videos by Kabat-Zinn:

1. Begin by getting yourself comfortable and allowing yourself to switch from your usual mode of doing to non-doing, to simply being.
2. Connect with your body and bring your attention to your breathing. Follow your breath as it comes in, and then out of your body, without trying to change it.
3. When you feel calm and ready to begin, bring to mind a person or a pet whom you are happy to see and for whom you have deep feelings of love. Imagine or sense this person or pet, noticing the feelings you have for them arise in your body. It may be a smile that spreads across your face. It may be a warmth in your body. Whatever it is, just enjoy feeling it.
4. Once you are steeping in the positive feelings that have arisen, hold on to those feelings but let the image of the person or pet in your mind's eye fade and be replaced with a reflection of yourself. Now offer loving-kindness to yourself, by whispering inwardly:
    *May I be safe.*
    *May I be happy.*
    *May I be healthy.*
    *May I live in peace, no matter what I am given.*
    *May my heart be filled with love and kindness.*

5. Notice the feelings and sensations that arise and let them be.
6. Next, try offering loving-kindness to someone you love. It can be a person from your past or present, living or dead. Bring that person to mind and whisper inwardly:

   *May you be safe.*
   *May you be happy.*
   *May you be healthy.*
   *May you live in peace, no matter what you are given.*
   *May your heart be filled with love and kindness.*

7. Notice the feelings and sensations that arise and let them be.
8. Once feelings for a loved one flow easily, turn your attention to someone with whom you have difficulty. With that person in mind, whisper inwardly:

   *May you be safe.*
   *May you be happy.*
   *May you be healthy.*
   *May you live in peace, no matter what you are given.*
   *May your heart be filled with love and kindness.*

9. Notice the feelings and sensations that arise, and see if you can just allow them, and let them be.

10. Lastly, bring to mind the broader community of which you are a part. Imagine your family, your neighbors and people across the globe. Fan out your attention until you include all living things and recite:

*May we be safe.*
*May we be happy.*
*May we be healthy.*
*May we live in peace, no matter what we are given.*
*May our hearts be filled with love and kindness.*

11. Notice the sensations and feelings that arise within you. Sit with them for a few moments until you are ready to end the meditation.

## Some tips for this meditation practice

You can rewrite the sentences according to your preference. Here is an example of a shorter version of the sentences, as they would be whispered for the first round:

*May I be happy.*
*May I be well.*
*May I be safe.*
*May I be peaceful and at ease.*

And an even shorter one:

*May I be happy, may I be healthy, may I be free from all pain.*

A tip for beginners for the round involving a person with whom you have difficulty is to start with someone relatively easy. Rather than the most difficult person, begin with someone who brings up feelings of slight annoyance or irritation. I also want to repeat a recommendation that applies to all meditation practices and that I find exceedingly helpful – if distracting thoughts arise, acknowledge them without becoming involved and return to the practice.

## SUMMARY

- A majority of people surveyed (in varying cultures) believe in and/or have experienced the feeling of being stared at.
- Research on scopaesthesia has been ongoing for over 100 years, with mixed outcomes, but positive results were found more recently with experiments measuring subconscious reactions to being looked at (electrodermal and gut-brain activity), though with no proven theory as to how this happens.
- Scientists have shown that plants and even isolated human cells react to positive/caring vibes sent from a short distance away (shown by electrical activity). Similarly, positive and negative vibes directed at a person's gut brain were also measured (shown by electrodermal activity).
- Loving-Kindness Meditation is a tried-and-tested practice for generating good vibes for yourself and for others.

# PART 2
# PLACES

Have you ever visited a new building or place and felt a strong positive – or negative – vibe the moment you walked in? This feeling is quite common, and something we often consciously look for. For example, people moving house often factor in "vibes" about a new potential home into their choices. Selecting a spot to spread out your picnic blanket might involve walking around and checking out several places until you find one that *feels* right, and there are many "places of power" – official and unofficial – around the world that are centers of worship or action, spiritual or secular.

In this part of the book, we'll be exploring the varied ways that people experience vibes associated with places and the science behind those experiences. Just as surrounding ourselves with positive and supportive people and vibes is a game-changer, likewise is our awareness of the vibrations of where we live and work, or places to recharge or uplift. And this knowledge stems back to ancient times. Creating a home sanctuary or visiting a place of worship or holy site can shift our mindset and influence our actions – just taking a walk in nature is a research-backed way to relieve tension or clear the mind. Recent research has demonstrated the health benefits of taking in the atmosphere of a forest, or forest bathing, including a study conducted in 24 forests across Japan that documented that spending time in forest environments promotes lower concentrations of the stress hormone cortisol plus a lower pulse rate and lower blood pressure than city environments (Park, et al., 2010).

Our environment directly affects our mood and emotions and influences our actions – but sometimes all is not as it seems. As with vibes from people, our reactions to some places are not necessarily what or why we'd expect. We'll explore some examples of situations where understanding the source of a vibe can be helpful, even life-saving, for making decisions about where you choose to spend your time, and places where things are not as you would believe.

## *What we will cover*

This part of the book discusses common places and situations where we experience vibes, or when we believe we are able to sense something extra from our environment:

- The experience of picking up vibes that feel as if they are left over from something that happened in a place before
- Haunted places

- Sensing spiritual vibes in a sacred place, like a church
- Feeling a deep connection with nature

On these topics, scientists have delved into the why and how, and come up with some remarkable findings which I'll share with you. I also provide a context for introducing simple methods effective for both changing your experience of vibes in places you visit and for influencing the vibes of a place for your own benefit.

# CHAPTER 5

## PICKING UP A VIBE WHEN YOU ENTER SOMEWHERE NEW

One of the most common situations when we "get a vibe" is when people have the feeling of some kind of energy, either positive or negative, as they enter a room or new place. Might this be explained by the physics of the space — the "local physics" — if it's possible that a house can hold on to traces of energy from the people who lived there before? If the prevailing emotions in the house were positive, a house may retain and emanate a warm, comforting vibe. If the prevailing emotions were negative, the house might perhaps feel cold and uninviting. Similarly, hostile vibes can sometimes be sensed at a location where violent events occurred.

The subtle energy that people are referring to in these situations can't be detected with current scientific instruments, so to solve the problem researchers and scientists have created experiments to detect the *effects* of this subtle energy instead and have had some success.

But before getting to these effects, we need to understand why places can have "vibes" due to some ordinary, unspectacular culprits.

## *Simple reasons for vibes*

Colors can influence the vibes of a place subconsciously and can be so impactful that there is an entire field of study termed "color psychology" dedicated to understanding how colors influence human behavior at a subconscious level. The famous Swiss psychiatrist Carl Jung is a major contributor to this field and many of the tenets of color psychology are used currently by companies as part of their marketing strategies. In a review of the literature relating to color psychology in the context of marketing, researchers at the University of Winnipeg in Canada found that colors can be effectively used to increase or decrease appetite, enhance mood, calm down customers, and reduce perception of waiting time (Singh, 2006). Most surprisingly, these researchers report that up to 90% of snap judgements made about products can be based on color alone.

Scientists outside the field of marketing have also investigated the impacts of color. For example, the color blue is supposed to cause people to feel relaxed and researchers at the Brain-Computer Interface Lab at the University of Granada tested this. They first put a small group of research participants under stress by giving them hard math problems while also instigating tension among them, and then letting them cool off alone in one of two relaxation rooms. During the relaxation session, the participants reclined in a comfortable puff-shaped seat inside a room specially designed for relaxation, originally used in schools as a time-out room for children with behavior disorders. One room had regular white lighting and the other had a very noticeable blue hue. The participants were instructed not to close their eyes (except for blinking) while they were relaxing. The super cool result was that being in a room bathed in blue lighting helps people calm down faster (Minguillon, et al., 2017).

Clutter can also be a huge contributor to the vibe of a place. I'll mention this here as another example of subconscious vibes influencing our behavior, and maybe something more.

While the principles of Feng Shui (pronounced "fung shway", the ancient Chinese art of arrangement) are based on the flow of the subtle energy qi, I believe that the armchair psychologist in most of us would agree that a messy space is a stressful space and that stress can generate negative vibes. It seems intuitively obvious that clutter can distract our attention away from what our focus should be on, causing our mind power to be scattered and us to feel stressed as a result. And we non-psychologists can pat ourselves on the back because it turns out that this amateur theory is endorsed by professional psychologists as well. Researchers at DePaul University and the University of New Mexico asked people about their wellbeing in relation to how much clutter they felt was in their homes. Participants were asked to rate how much they agreed with statements such as "the clutter in my home upsets me" and "I have to move things in order to accomplish tasks in my home". The researchers found a strong link between clutter problems and both life dissatisfaction and procrastination, especially among older adults (Ferrari and Roster, 2018). Another study by researchers at UCLA found a correlation between the amount of clutter in a home and increased levels of a stress hormone in the blood throughout the day (Saxbe and Repetti, 2010).

Professional psychologists have also unearthed interesting findings about our reactions to the stuff around us. My favorite example of this was reported by researchers at Stanford and Yale Universities studying the effects of material priming on judgement and behavioral choices (Kay, et al., 2004). Let me explain.

I refer to this study as the "briefcase versus backpack" experiment. It showed that if volunteers were put in a room that contained objects commonly associated with business – for example, a briefcase – they acted more competitively than when they were sitting next to a backpack. In the researchers' language, the volunteers were subconsciously primed to exhibit more competitive behavior. What this means for us in our homes is that some of the clutter there could be doing more than just distracting us and scattering our mind power. Objects that we associate with acting a certain way can nudge us into acting that way without us even realizing it. Medication bottles left out could be a small but persistent drag on our feelings about our health and diminish our vim and vigor, for example. An ever-growing stack of unopened mail on the kitchen table could result in an out-of-control mindset. Luggage might keep you feeling on the go and never quite settled at home.

## *Subtle energy and emotional residue*

The theory of emotional residue posits that people's thoughts and emotions can somehow leave traces of subtle energy in the physical environment (also known as an "energy trace"), which can later influence others or be sensed by others. Researchers at the Columbia Business School came up with this name and conducted a series of cross-cultural experiments examining beliefs in emotional residue among people in India and the US – basically asking them if they believe in it – and found that this concept seems to be intuitively felt by people in both countries (Savani, et al., 2011). In another study they tested whether people's beliefs in emotional residue could influence their choices. In the choice experiment, they had participants fill out a sham survey that was irrelevant. The researchers were just watching which of two rooms the participants would choose to go into to take the survey. The sign on the door of one room implied that people in the room before had spent time in there recalling happy life events. The sign on the other door indicated that people had recently been in there recalling *unhappy* life events. The result was that the majority of both Indians and Americans chose to go into the room where they thought that the previous occupants had been recalling happy memories. At some level, they felt that it mattered and chose to fill out their surveys in the room where any possible residual effects would be from happy emotions.

These emotional residue experiments show that many of us believe in the possibility that mysterious energy traces – vibes – from people can be left behind in places. The first time I saw evidence supporting this theory in my lab was when I was studying energy medicine healers (as part of a cancer research project funded by the US National Institutes of Health) and received some advice from William A. Tiller, Professor Emeritus of the Department of Material Sciences and Engineering at Stanford University. Dr Tiller is one of the most prominent scientists whose research supports the idea that space can be affected, or "conditioned," by people's vibes. Tiller and his colleagues believe that physical properties of a space can be altered by people activating units of consciousness of the space. (In technical language, they theorize that human intentions can influence materials in space through a higher level of physical reality, involving a change in the electromagnetic gauge symmetry state of that space (Tiller, et al., 2004)). Dr Tiller threw this theory in my face, in a collegial way, when I was a rookie in the field giving a presentation about my experiments with energy medicine healers. I was lamenting my inability to replicate the results of published experiments reporting that these professional healers could promote the growth of human cells in Petri dishes from a short distance by manipulating subtle energy (Taft, Moore, et al., 2005; Taft, Nieto, et al., 2005).

Tiller wasn't my only heckler in the audience. I was presenting to a group of scientists convened to talk about energy medicine research and I was the only one presenting negative results. Some of the reactions I got didn't seem to ring true to me. Reactions like "the healers in your experiments weren't powerful enough" seemed off the mark, because I was working with highly qualified energy medicine practitioners. Tiller's remark, on the other hand, struck me as worth considering. He suggested that the obvious reason that I could not get replicable results with these healers was that my laboratory was full of bad vibes, due to the concurrent experiments that I was running in the same space involving chemotherapy and radiation. According to him, these brutal Western anticancer agents were creating "negative" energy in my laboratory such that the subtle manipulations of the healing energy were being drowned out. They were like bulldozers ploughing all over a field where delicate seedlings were trying to grow, and the ruts in the mud remained and got worse each time they drove through. Energetically, by the time I brought these healers in, my laboratory was like a vibes war zone. He challenged me to try the experiment again in a location that was prepared energetically – a "conditioned" space. By this he meant a space that had been steeped in positive vibes over time so that the physical properties would be conducive to the flow of subtle healing energy. So, I set out to do just that.

## *Laboratory experiments on conditioning space*

My colleague at IONS, Dean Radin, offered for us to set the experiment up inside an electromagnetically shielded chamber on the IONS campus in nearby Petaluma. This chamber was an 8' x 8' x 8' enclosure made of steel plates that reminded me of a space capsule, with a door that closed with a long, pivoting metal bar. Its nickname was "The Box" and it seemed the perfect location for our space-conditioning experiment.

We set up a three-day experiment with human brain cell cultures being treated with healing intention each day. The healers never touched the Petri dishes and the experimental procedures also included untreated cell cultures to serve as the control condition. The treatment on the first day was in The Box before any conditioning of the space by the healers, when it was still a clean slate. Once the first batch of cells was treated and taken out, four healers went to work conditioning the space by conducting hours of praying, chanting and healing, on and off for three days. Our hypothesis was that the brain cells would respond by growing more than the control cells as the experiment progressed and the vibes inside The Box became conditioned.

What Dr Radin didn't tell the rest of the team at the beginning of the experiment was that he had secretly placed a random number generator inside The Box. Random number generators are devices designed to continuously spit out random numbers, like robotic coin flippers or dice rollers. They are extraordinarily reliable at being random because they are typically used in high-stakes situations that require the production of unpredictable numbers. Researchers use random number generators to test for the effects of subtle energy by placing them in a location and then watching to see if the streams of numbers coming out start to become more predictable (using a p-value, as I explained earlier). The idea is that subtle energy vibes concentrated in a location could cause a type of coherence in the local physics and this coherence could influence the devices to behave more coherently, or less randomly.

Dr Radin's secret hypothesis was that if the accumulation of healing vibes inside The Box were to build up such that the cells could respond, then the machines might pick up on that "conditioning" too and start behaving in a more orderly manner. It turned out that the results supported both our official hypothesis and Dr Radin's covert experiment (Radin, et al., 2004). The brain cells treated with healing energy didn't seem to be affected by treatments on the first and second day. But on the third day, their growth was significantly increased compared to the untreated control cells. Likewise, the numbers streaming out of the random number generators became significantly less random on the third day. We were excited by these results, especially because this was the first space-conditioning experiment to examine biological and mechanical targets simultaneously and the statistical analyses of both targets was very encouraging.

With the brain cells, the statistics produced a p-value of $p = 0.02$. In non-statistics language, if you were to repeat the same experiment 100 times, and the healing intention had no effect whatsoever, you could still expect to see this level of cell growth stimulation in just two out of the 100 experiments. The random number generator results scored a $p = 0.00009$, meaning you could expect to see this level of non-randomness in 0.009 of 100 experiments (or a mere 9 out 100,000 experiments), if it were just by chance.

These data provide compelling evidence suggesting that the healing intentions of the energy healers were able to change the local physics inside The Box, and they add to a growing body of evidence that little microclimates of slightly changed physics can be induced due to people's intense emotions or focused attention.

## *Field experiments on altering local physics*

A small number of pioneering scientists and engineers are finding evidence supporting the possibility that our physical reality can get slightly warped in a specific place due to people's intense emotions or focused attention. They theorise that coherence in a group of people's thoughts or emotions can cause coherence in the physical reality of the surrounding space. "Coherent consciousness creates order in the world," is one of their mantras (https://noosphere. princeton.edu/). The primary way that they test this theory of altering the local physics is by placing random number generators in the spaces to see if the randomness decreases when the consciousness of nearby humans becomes more coherent – and the results have been compelling.

The largest effort in this regard has been the Global Consciousness Project, which has meticulously documented the output of a network of random number generators spread around the world. There are currently about 70 host sites in the network, and at each one, random data streams are recorded continuously, one trial per second, day after day flowing into a central database for analysis. The researchers test whether there are departures from expected random output from the machines during global events when great numbers of people experience shared emotion or intention. For example, they looked for deviations in the random data produced by machines across the globe before, during and after the terrorist attack on the Twin Towers in New York City on September 11, 2001, and saw a significant deviation in the behavior of the machines during that event (Nelson, et al., 2002), which supports the idea of the local physics being altered where the machines were operating. Snowballing on top of that, the results of numerous analyses like this compiled over more than a decade have produced similar results and strongly support the reality of a connection between coherent human consciousness and less random behavior from machines that normally behave randomly. The probability that the effect could be just a chance fluctuation is less than one in a trillion (Jahn, et al., 2007).

## Why do a place's vibes matter?

As we've seen, the subconscious vibes people pick up in a place can nudge them into acting in certain ways and even influence their decisions. Some states in the

US have laws that home sellers must disclose if there has been a death on the property within a certain time period, and the briefcase versus backpack experiment demonstrated that people acted in different ways when placing different kinds of things around them. Clearly paying attention to a place's vibes is something to consider as a potential advantage or disadvantage.

I also shared results of Petri dish experiments suggesting that the influence can work in the reverse direction – that people's vibes can affect a place.

The research is far from complete but the results so far make a strong case that the vibes people emit can alter the local physics of a place, affecting what happens in that space. Data suggests that generating positive vibes in a place can make it more conducive for healing – the experiments investigating this possibility discussed above involved the coordinated intentions of trained healers but the clear implication is anybody could condition a space without any special training.

## *Clearing bad vibes*

Clearly any practical methods to change the vibes of somewhere could really impact our lives. Here are a couple of techniques for "normal" people to use on "normal" days to influence a place's vibe. These methods were developed long before modern science started poking around the topic of vibes and they are still being practiced by people around the globe today.

Smudging is traditionally a sacred ceremony where herbs are burnt to cleanse the subtle energies of a person or place. Over recent years, smudging places has become widely popular – the *New York Times* recently reported on the industry of smudgers, branded as "space clearers," that has emerged within the real estate industry (Haughney, 2011). It has become trendy for people to want to chase out any negative vibes from their new home to make room for good ones.

## *Smudging*

Smudging is a simple way to influence the vibes of your room, home or workplace, clearing the space and inviting in positive energy. Perhaps you're feeling sluggish in your job and want to clear your office, or you want to freshen your space after the end of a relationship.

To conduct a smudging ritual of your own, you'll need a herb bundle, matches and a fire-proof container. Excellent herbs to use for the ritual include cedar, bay, rosemary, lavender and white sage, and you can purchase smudge sticks online and at specialist stores.

Here is a simple practice for smudging a room using herbs:

1. Open a door or window to create an exit route for the bad vibes (and also the smoke).
2. Position yourself in the center or at the front door of the room and adopt an attitude of calm.
3. Set your intention by determining what you want to release from the space. Then, decide on a prayer, mantra or affirmation – a simple phrase or statement that is repeated – that sums up this intention. An example shared by third-generation Native American medicine woman, Koa Mikaelah (www.heliosandsolene.com), is: *"I intend to manifest happiness naturally."*
4. Light the herb bundle using a match or candle while holding it tilted at an angle. Let it burn for one to ten seconds, so that embers take hold.
5. Fan the herb gently, either by hand or with a feather, to encourage a steady stream of smoke and imagine that the smoke has the power to absorb negative energy and carry it away.
6. Cleanse yourself first by swirling the herb bundle at arm's length to allow the smoke to waft over your entire body, working its way up from your feet. You may or may not choose to recite a

prayer, mantra or affirmation (either internally or aloud) that is specific to smudging yourself, such as: *"I am grounded and calm."*

7. Begin reciting the prayer, mantra or affirmation (either internally or aloud) and continue doing so over and over for the duration of the ritual.

8. Next, walk slowly around the room in a clockwise direction while swirling the herb to encourage the smoke to waft around into every nook and cranny of the room, including toward the ceiling.

9. Once you've made our way back to your starting position, press the burning tip of the herb bundle firmly into the fire-proof container until the smoke no longer rises. Do not extinguish the herb with water (this makes a difference as to how the herb bundle lights up the next time).

10. Express gratitude (either internally or aloud) in any way that feels right to you.

## *Changing the vibes of a space by moving things around*

The arrangement of stuff in a space can have a profound impact on the vibe people experience in it. This is sometimes easy to sense on an intuitive level for many of us, for example when rearranging furniture in a room makes the space feel clearer and more uplifting, but Feng Shui turns it into an art form. As mentioned on page 99, Feng Shui is based on the belief that the arrangement of objects in our environment can affect our emotions and wellbeing by affecting the flow of the subtle energy known as qi. This practice was developed in ancient China and made its way to the West after the end of the Chinese Cultural Revolution in the 1970s.

Modern attempts to scientifically verify that Feng Shui works are scarce and have yielded mixed results. An international collaboration of researchers, from Cornell University and Delft University of Technology in the Netherlands, assessed patients' experiences of healthcare waiting rooms that included properly placed Feng Shui elements and found positive results. They concluded that fostering and encouraging a holistic approach to comfort utilizing eastern and western concepts and ergonomic principles creates a sense of "placeness" and balance (Bazley, et al., 2016). On the other hand, a group of researchers from the United Kingdom designed a study to test whether applying Feng Shui principles to critical care bed spaces would improve the emotional wellbeing of the nurses that worked with them and were unable to demonstrate any such effect (Charles, et al., 2017).

It is important to keep in mind that the original practice has been significantly morphed to be more palatable to Westerners. A quick search online will yield plenty of do-it-yourself instructions for Feng Shui-ing your home but be advised that often the authentic core principles and techniques are lost. Your best bet is to hire a Feng Shui consultant who is a member of an officially recognized Feng Shui organization (such as the International Feng Shui Guild and the International Feng Shui Association) to assure you regarding their training, experience and standards of professional practice.

An authentic Feng Shui consultation involves complicated calculations that take into account a floor plan drawn to scale, the dates of birth of the occupants, and the date of the building's construction, in addition to an analysis of the flow of qi according to Feng Shui principles such as the Five Elements. The Five Elements principle describes how everything in the universe comes from five elements – metal, water, wood, fire and earth – and balancing them within a space can balance the flow of qi in a space. I imagine there will still be some readers that want to give it a try on their own so I'll offer two fail-safe baby steps you can take that will give a taste of the resulting improved vibes and convince you to hire a professional so that you can achieve the full effect.

Step number one is to declutter your place. Decluttering may seem too basic to be part of ancient art but I guarantee the professionals will tell you that clearing away clutter is imperative and a step that cannot be skipped. Using the metaphor of flowing water for qi, you don't want unnecessary things blocking the flow of energy and leading to stagnant qi. The simplest version of decluttering is to get rid of all unnecessary things by putting them away or disposing of them. Some tips for this method are to make sure you clean every corner and discard items that are broken, stress you out or are negative reminders – all things that impart anxiety. Two lovely books that offer sagacious help specifically for this baby step are *Clutter Busting Your Life: Clearing Physical and Emotional Clutter to Reconnect with Yourself and Others* by Brooks Palmer (Palmer, 2012) and *The Life-Changing Magic of Tidying Up* by Marie Kondo (Kondo, 2014).

Step number two is to locate and then plan around what is called the "Commanding Position" in a room. To locate the Commanding Position, consider how you will use the room because this spot should be where you spend most of your time in that room. For a bedroom, it will be the spot for the bed; for an office, it will be the spot for the desk, and so on. One important guideline is to choose a Commanding Position that is furthest from the door and allows a clear view of the door. According to Feng Shui theory, a clear line of sight to the door will appease your state of inner vigilance, regardless of whether or not you are aware of it. It is also recommended you choose a spot not directly opposite the door. In the example of a bedroom, the head of the bed should be placed against the wall opposite the door, and it should either be positioned diagonally in the corner opposite the door or to the right or the left of the door.

Once you have located the Commanding Position and placed the dominant or most-used piece of furniture in it, you can arrange the remaining furniture and décor in a way that feels most natural and comfortable to you. Just imagine how the arrangement would affect the flow of subtle energy in the room. After all, one of the primary goals of Feng Shui is for people to feel comfortable and nurtured in a space so it makes sense that how you feel in the place is a legitimate indicator of whether you are getting it right.

# SUMMARY

- Subconscious vibes from the use of color are shown to influence the vibes of a place – color psychology is its own field of study.
- Clutter in a space is also shown to induce subconscious vibes, and significant research has proven a strong connection between clutter and life dissatisfaction, plus physiological results such as the increased levels of stress hormone in the blood.
- The simple presence of objects in our environment can subconsciously influence and prime us and affect behavior. Our belief in potential emotional residue in a place also affects behavior.
- Experimental data suggests that energy healers were able to change the local physics of a positively conditioned place, and there is growing evidence that microclimates of slightly changed physics can be induced by people's intense emotions or focused attention.
- Methods we can use to affect the vibes in a place include:
  - Smudging
  - Feng Shui

# CHAPTER 6

---

# HAUNTED PLACES

We've talked about when people experience good vibes or bad vibes in places. This chapter drills down into some of the most extreme cases of feeling *bad* vibes in a place – instances such as the "haunted house" and other places that people avoid for fear of ghosts or something bad. Beliefs in ghosts is prevalent cross-culturally, including in contemporary Western cultures (Jacobi, 2003; Baker and Bader, 2014). A recent estimation of the prevalence of the belief in ghosts among Americans found that nearly half of Americans believe in ghosts and as many as 18% will go so far as to say that they have had contact with a ghost (Stierwalt, 2019).

So, what is the source of these spooky vibes? The common assumption is that a supernatural spirit has somehow crossed the boundary of the living and the dead. I won't attempt to refute this possibility. Instead, I'll review some of the studies that have looked into possible alternative explanations – namely, unseen environmental factors triggering subconscious vibes that are experienced as fearful feelings.

While these explanations are not as fantastical as horror films, they are great examples of why paying attention to vibes matters. In some situations, an awareness of these kinds of bad vibes could actually keep you out of physical danger. The methods shared later in this chapter test your environment to see whether or not you might be in one of those dangerous situations.

## *Boston haunted house*

One of the earliest scientific reports regarding a haunted house was published in a very prestigious research journal over 100 years ago (Schneider, 1913). It was the case of a haunted house in the Back Bay area of Boston in 1913. The author of the report wrote:

*"The trouble centered in the third and fourth stories, which were occupied by the children and servants – the slumber of whom were disturbed by strange sensations. It was said to be a common occurrence for servants to awake in the night with a sensation of oppression, 'as if someone were tapping upon me,' or with a 'creepy feeling going all over me with a feeling of being paralyzed.'*

*Sounds were also said to be heard, as if someone were walking about the house. . . . A little boy, for example, awoke one night and inquired of his nurse why she had been lying on him. . . . The children appeared sluggish in the morning and pale, even cold water losing its power to enliven them. . .*

*On investigation it appeared that previous tenants had been troubled in the same way, matters having reached the point where the servants talked of seeing walking apparitions. The present occupant, although not entertaining any vitalistic theory of the phenomena, was fully alive to the reality and gravity of the situation, and anxious to find the underlying cause."*

And this was discovered: it became apparent there was a leak from a "viciously defective hot-air furnace" resulting in the inhabitants of the upper floors of the house being bathed in an atmosphere of flue gasses. Once the furnace was replaced, the trouble ceased.

## A modern "haunting"

Before she became a journalist, Carrie Poppy moved into a new place in Los Angeles and quickly developed the impression that she was being "haunted by an evil spirit." It started with vague, creepy feelings as if she wasn't alone in the house. Then the sensations started to get more intense and scarier. She would hear weird sounds and feel a physical pressure on her chest. She gives a great TED Talk in which she tells the story of her fear mounting to the point that she felt desperate and she called a friend for advice (Poppy, 2017). Her friend told her to burn sage to chase away any evil spirits. She did this but it had no effect. Then she searched the Internet for advice and found a forum of "ghostbusters" who asked her if she had checked to see if there might be a carbon monoxide leak in her home. She called the gas company and a technician came to her home with a carbon monoxide detector. It turned out that she was experiencing carbon monoxide poisoning. This experience inspired her to become an investigative journalist with a flair for critical-yet-kind examinations of paranormal claims.

Carbon monoxide is a gas made when fuel burns and breathing too much of it can cause all of the feelings that Carrie Poppy and the Bostonians in the 1900s were feeling and more, including headache, dizziness, disorientation, confusion, auditory hallucinations, chest and muscle pain, and unexplained feelings of dread. If you keep breathing in too much, it can cause coma and death. The gas company technician told Poppy that she was lucky that she called when she did because she could have died. These two cases of gas leaks resulting in people feeling like their house was haunted illustrate a curious case of subconscious vibes – unconscious somatic influences again as the nervous system reacts to signals in the environment (as discussed earlier when looking at ways we instinctively judge new people we meet). Carbon monoxide is an invisible and odorless gas, so our eyes and nose can't alert us to the danger. Instead, our bodies react to its presence.

You can easily test for the presence of carbon monoxide in your home by installing an inexpensive carbon monoxide detector or by using a commercially available indoor air quality test that includes carbon monoxide testing. You can also pay service companies to perform indoor air quality tests and some utility companies and fire departments will come to your home and check for carbon monoxide for free.

## Conjuring up ghosts in the lab

Another case of the non-supernatural induction of creepy feelings has been shown in the lab. Neuroscientists discovered that the sensed presence of a "sentient being" in the room with you when there's nobody there can be evoked by applying magnetic fields to specific parts of the brain. A study conducted at Laurentian University in Canada brought students into the lab and had them sit in a quiet room with a device next to their heads that could generate focused magnetic fields but didn't tell them if or when the device was turned on. The scientists who interacted with the students also didn't know if or when the device was turned on (double-blind conditions). Those scientists controlling the magnetic field generator did so in four different ways: three applying very weak magnetic fields, primarily over the temporoparietal region of the brain, and one was a "sham" condition with no magnetic field applied. This temporoparietal region is approximately just above your ears on both sides of your head and is associated with the sense of self, along with many other mental functions. The magnetic fields were applied to either the right side, the left side or both sides for 20 minutes. The students who received greater magnetic stimulation over the right side of the brain or equal stimulation across both sides reported more frequent incidences of sensed presences, fears, and odd smells than the subjects who received greater stimulation over the left side, or who were exposed to the sham-field condition (Persinger, 1993). These results, along with similar results from other labs (Cook and Persinger, 1997; Booth, et al., 2005; St-Pierre and Persinger, 2006; Meli and Persinger, 2009), have led to the hypothesis that the magnetic stimulation is activating parts of the brain that control our sense of self in weird ways – causing the experiences attributed to visitations by ghosts and other ephemeral phenomena.

# *Haunted palace*

A field study conducted at Hampton Court Palace, considered one of the most haunted places in England, found a connection between naturally occurring magnetic fields in different rooms of the castle and reports of spooky feelings (Wiseman, et al., 2002). This study, led by Richard Wiseman at the University of Hertfordshire in England, brought participants to areas within the Palace with a considerable reputation for being haunted and asked them to quietly walk around and note if they experienced anything unusual. They were asked to place one or more crosses on a floor plan to indicate where any experience(s) occurred, write a brief description of any experience(s) and indicate whether they believed that their experience(s) were due to a ghost. The mapping of the magnetic fields in the castle was done in a blinded fashion – that is the scientist who set up and operated the magnetic field sensors was not aware of the number of unusual experiences reported for each room. Results showed that, even though participants who said that they believed in ghosts reported significantly more spooky feelings than disbelievers (more on this below), both groups reported significantly more of these feelings in rooms with increased levels of magnetic field strength and field variance (the difference between the direction of the Earth's magnetic field lines and true north). While it was not directly tested, it is conceivable that the magnetic field exposure in the Palace rooms resulted in brain regions associated with the sense of self being stimulated in a similar way as was achieved in the lab studies described above.

## *The case of inaudible sound*

Infrasound is another invisible environmental factor that may explain some "hauntings" because it too can cause seemingly mysterious, disturbing feelings. Sound waves at frequencies lower than the lowest bass sound that we can hear are called infrasound. Even though our ears don't detect these sound waves, our bodies and minds can be affected by them. Psychologists at the University of Hertfordshire demonstrated in an experiment that high levels of infrasound can give people creepy vibes, just like carbon monoxide poisoning. They conducted their experiment during concerts at a renowned performance venue in central London. Some of the songs were infused with high-level infrasound and some weren't. Without revealing anything about the special addition to some of the songs, the researchers asked the audience to describe their reactions to the music. The results were analyzed in a double-blind fashion and showed that nearly a quarter of the concert goers reported more unusual experiences when the song was infused with infrasound. The unusual experiences included sorrow, anxiety, dread and shivers down the spine, along with other feelings of unease (Wiseman, 2008).

Strange effects of infrasound were also demonstrated in a controlled laboratory experiment at Coventry University. This experiment was inspired by the experience of researchers working in a medical lab at the university who suspected that the lab had become haunted. They had suddenly started to experience cold sweats and feelings of dread and depression. The story goes that the head of the lab even started seeing ghosts when working late in the lab. On investigation they discovered that a recently installed exhaust fan was pumping high levels of infrasound into the lab at about a 19 Hertz frequency. Once they tinkered with the fan, the ghosts and related scary stuff vanished. That was a pretty convincing resolution but they wanted to be scientific about it so they recreated the conditions with infrasound generators in the lab to see if the scary stuff would come back. They did and the results were published in the *Journal of the Society for Psychical Research* (Tandy and Lawrence, 1998). The same team also confirmed that there were high levels of infrasound at Warwick Castle, another famously haunted place in England (Tandy and Lawrence, 2004).

Testing for infrasound in your home is not as easy as testing for carbon monoxide. Infrasound is almost always in our environment and low levels of it are not a problem; there is plenty of benevolent infrasound going around. Cats produce infrasound when they purr on your lap (purring produces both sound that we can hear and sound that we can't hear). Our hearts produce infrasound when they beat.

The sources of toxic levels of infrasound tend to be industrial sites with heavy rotating machinery, much more so than in homes. You can get an infrasound detecting device or app for a smartphone, however, interpreting the data from the app is more complicated than an alarm going off when carbon monoxide is detected because infrasound comes in a range of frequencies and intensities. The simplest rule of thumb is to set the units of measurement to "dBz" (which stands for decibels with zero-weighting) and check that the value doesn't exceed 80 dBz, the recommended maximum threshold for chronic exposure (Chaban, et al., 2021).

## *Scary movies*

Filmmakers have taken advantage of the fear factor of the close cousin of infrasound, the lowest of the low bass sound that we *can* hear, to augment the scariness of horror films. These sonic vibrations are neighbors to infrasound on the sonic frequency map, right at the edge of where most humans can still hear. Remember that the frequency that was spooking everybody in the lab was 19 Hertz? Well, it turns out that if you shift up a little bit to 27 Hertz, just past the threshold where it can be heard, some of the spooky vibe-inducing effects are still there. This became apparent when Gaspar Noe's film *Irreversible* played at the 2002 Cannes Film Festival in France. He had laced the first 30 minutes of the soundtrack with 27 Hertz sound and some of the viewers were scared so badly that they vomited. The BBC ran the headline: "Cannes Film Sickens Audience" noting that "fire wardens had to administer oxygen to 20 people who fainted during the film," (BBC News, 2002).

## *The power of suggestion*

Aside from spooky vibes, the power of suggestion is a factor that has shown up in investigations of supernatural phenomena like ghost sightings.

Researchers at the University of Illinois analyzed over 900 "ghostly" experiences and found that approximately 60% of reports mentioned some form of prior suggestion that the location was haunted (e.g., rumors, advertising or prior knowledge of previous experiences reported in the location) (Lange, et al., 1996). They then set up an experiment to specifically test for the power of suggestion to induce paranormal-type experiences. They asked two groups of participants to walk around a run-down building that used to be a cinema and fill out a questionnaire about psychological and physiological perceptions. Before entering the building, one group was told that the cinema had been the site of reports of paranormal activity and the other was told that the building was currently under renovation and the experiment was about people's reaction to the environment in general. As predicted, the "paranormal" group reported significantly more physical, emotional, psychic, and mystical experiences than those in the "renovation" group (Lange and Houran, 1997).

Interestingly, the investigation at Hampton Court Palace that measured magnetic fields also put the potential influence of suggestion under the microscope and found the opposite result (Wiseman, et al. 2002). Before entering the supposedly haunted areas of the Palace, participants were given an orientation talk in the Prince of Wales Closet – a quiet area of the Palace not usually open to the public. Half of them were told the area they were going to walk through had recently been associated with an increased number of reports of unusual experiences (this was the "positive suggestion" condition), while the other half were told that very few people had recently experienced anything unusual in the area ("negative suggestion" condition). Wiseman and colleagues had predicted that the participants in the "positive suggestion" condition would report more unusual experiences but that didn't happen. The suggestion manipulation had no significant effect on the number of unusual experiences the participants reported or the degree to which they were attributed to a ghost.

Despite the contrary results from the Hampton Court Palace experiment, numerous studies over the past 20 years have found evidence supporting the possibility that expectations can become self-fulfilling prophesies by producing psychosomatic phenomena when visiting haunted places (Dagnal, et al., 2020). These factors can make it difficult to discern whether or not a creepy feeling you are picking up is a signal from your body telling you something important about your environment (subconscious vibes) or just your imagination running away with itself – or, of course, a real disembodied entity.

# SUMMARY

- The influence of haunting-type episodes is widespread, with multiple sources. Science has failed to evidence supernatural links, but have found evidence of spooky vibes and occurrences as a form of subconscious vibes alert on dangerous environmental conditions such as carbon monoxide and flue gas leaks.
- Infrasound is another invisible environmental factor that may explain some hauntings as these low sound waves can cause disturbing feelings and physiological effects.
- Scientists have managed to induce creepy feelings in the lab by applying magnetic fields to specific parts of the brain leading to the sensation of being in the presence of a "sentient being".
- Experiments at Hampton Court Palace also showed a correlation between magnetic fields in certain rooms and spooky sensations.
- Another non-vibe factor to consider is the power of suggestion and belief:

    - Those with a prior belief in the paranormal tend to be primed to notice ghostly phenomena.
    - Ghost-believers interpret unusual experiences as being caused by ghosts.

# CHAPTER 7

---

# SENSING SPIRITUAL
# VIBES IN A PLACE

Now let's shift our attention to some extremely good vibes. This chapter is about the places where people feel spiritual vibes: shrines, mosques, temples, churches and other places of worship are notable in this regard. I'll also discuss non-religious sites because the definition of spiritual vibes that I'm adopting for this chapter is not limited to people's notions of God or a higher power. By spiritual vibe, I'm referring to a particular type of superconscious vibe that induces self-transcendence, where the self is experienced as fundamentally related or interconnected with the divine or all that is.

I'll share my belief that *any place* could be a location to experience this type of vibe, and some esoteric concepts from scholars that have informed my ideas about this topic. The method I'll share is a meditation practice that I find helpful for tapping into spiritual vibes wherever I am.

# Sagrada Família
## *(Holy Family Church)*

Barcelona's Basílica de la Sagrada Família, or Sagrada Família, was designed by the Catalan architect Antoni Gaudí and is one of the most spectacular buildings ever constructed by man. By all accounts, it is a place that inspires spiritual vibes regardless of one's religio-cultural worldview.

Gaudí was famous for creating buildings in harmony with nature's shapes and forms and this unique emphasis is very much in evidence. The free-form, organic flow of the exterior of the church intensifies dramatically on the inside. The massive columns holding up the ceiling looked like a forest of majestic trees, with branches and leaves bejeweled by the colors streaming through the stained-glass windows to create an appropriate mood for prayer and reflection.

Religious association is a key element for many when they feel spiritual vibes in a place and the Sagrada Família has this in spades. Pope Benedict XVI bestowed the Vatican's highest honour on the church, transforming it into a basilica, which is considered a sacred place forever. The breathtaking building also expresses a religious association with its exterior telling the story of Jesus. One of the reasons Gaudí planned the facades this way was because many of the working class were illiterate at the time and he wanted to provide them with a "Bible made of stone."

## *Profane spaces are good for spiritual vibes too*

Whether a magnificent basilica or a regular old church, feelings of deep interconnectedness abound in places where some relationship has been established between that location and the divine, creating a boundary between the sacred space and the external profane world. But the type of spiritual vibes that I am talking about also abound in secular spaces. For these spaces, a key element is an association with ritual or ceremony.

Stonehenge is an example of somewhere famous for emitting spiritual vibes where religious association is not a key element. Modern pagans make a pilgrimage to this Neolithic stone circle near Salisbury in England for solstice ceremonies and many of the hundreds of thousands of tourists that pour through it on the rest of the days of the year say that they feel spiritual energy there. Maybe this is a case where emotional residue plays a part as pagans have been conducting ceremonies at Stonehenge for hundreds of years? Or perhaps their thoughts and emotions have saturated the place with traces of subtle energy that can be sensed at some level today as spiritual vibes?

The acoustics of Stonehenge could also contribute to people's tendency to feel spiritual vibes. Sound researchers analyzed models of the structure as it was before it fell into ruin and found a powerful low frequency resonance at around 47 Hertz produced by the unique arrangement of the mammoth stones when low frequency sound was introduced, such as drumming (Till, 2019). This is not as low as the 27 Hertz sound infused into the soundtrack of the Gaspar Noe's horror film, but it's pretty close. It may have given the space an otherworldly character, helping to induce spiritual vibes. Sound researchers have made similar claims based on tests conducted inside the pyramids of Giza (Hale and Campbell, 2007).

## *DIY sacred space*

"Do-it-yourself" sacred space is the best example of a place where you can enjoy spiritual vibes without a religious association. This could be a designated space in your home for rituals like meditation or yoga or just a space that helps you "touch base" with feelings of deep interconnectedness on a daily basis. If you are able to designate space in your home, place objects there that you feel give you positive energy and inspire you.

Consider using a screen or other boundary to make your sacred space feel more contained, relaxing and personal. When away from home, you can create pop-up sacred spaces with a little intention and creativity – bring sentimental items from your home to act as touchstones to the peaceful feelings of your home sanctuary.

## *The place is not the most important ingredient*

The Sagrada Família, Stonehenge, the pyramids of Giza, the meditation corner in your bedroom and other places designated for ritual and ceremony may nudge people toward experiencing spiritual vibes but the ultimate key is letting the concept of separateness dissipate. Open yourself up to experiencing spiritual vibes by letting go of all ideas of yourself as separate from other people and other things in the world – *no matter where you are* and you "get to a place" where it feels as if you are part of the vibrations of the underlying fabric of reality that connects everything.

The most helpful advice I've received is that quieting the mind is a great first step. Pausing the mind's chatter makes it easier for our attention to expand beyond the confines of "self" as separate from others. This view is supported by the writings of Eckhart Tolle, the contemporary German mystic. Tolle emphasizes that thoughts are concepts in your conscious field, but they're not you. Moreover, he defines a spiritual awakening as the moment when you realize that you are not your thoughts (Tolle, 1997). Figure 5 below demonstrates the attempt to get to a place where you can unblock your experience of spiritual vibes.

The strategy is simply to take a break from your thoughts. The inner circle in the figure represents our thinking world, the "X" marking the spot where your attention is focused and what your awareness is occupied with in the present moment. I've left the larger circle unlabeled because it is tricky for me to name a place that is outside of thought. To use the nomenclature from the English writer Alan Watts, I would label it "Real World" and this is where I believe we access spiritual vibes.

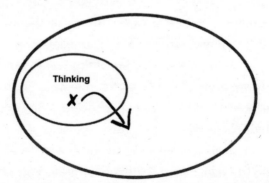

Figure 5. Map to a "Place" Where You Can Feel Spiritual Vibes.

## "Dumping Buckets" meditation

Meditation is one of innumerable techniques for bumping your attention out of the thinking bubble, and there are many types of meditation. I've selected a meditation practice that involves giving your mind something to do, as opposed to the type of meditation where you aspire to just let it go.

I learned this qigong meditation practice called "Dumping Buckets" from Master Weijong Fu, a qigong teacher in Beijing, over two decades ago and I practice it on a regular basis. Other branches of Traditional Chinese Medicine based on manipulating qi include acupuncture (physical manipulation) and herbal remedies (chemical manipulation). The idea of the Dumping Buckets meditation is to imagine a drop of water trickling down your skin so that your mind stimulates the flow of qi throughout your whole body. I learned this practice as a daily meditation aimed at promoting mental and physical health but I noticed as I practiced that it had a powerful muting effect on my inner voices.

These are the basic steps for Dumping Buckets meditation, taught to me by Master Fu:

1. Sit in a chair with your legs uncrossed, feet flat on the floor, and your arms and hands resting either on your legs or in your lap. If possible, try not

to lean against the back of the chair. Keep your back straight, yet relaxed. You can also do this lying down.

2. Close your eyes and imagine a water source. It could be the ocean, a waterfall, or a lake that you used to swim in as a child, or any body of water that you feel good about.

3. Imagine reaching out and scooping up a bucketful of the water. This will be the first of three buckets that you scoop up.

4. Lift the bucket up and tip it gently so that, in your mind's eye, a drop of the water falls onto the top of your head. Focus all your attention on the feeling of the water touching your scalp – however that feels to you.

5. Following the feeling of the water as it slowly travels down the front of your body. Follow it as it trickles across your forehead, eyes, nose, lips, chin, neck, chest, belly and private parts. Let the drop split into two, one to travel down each of your legs.

6. Along the way, if your thoughts start back up and grab your attention away, simply acknowledge them and redirect your attention to the water. You can either continue on from the same spot where your thoughts intruded or restart that drop at the top of your head. Either way is good.

7. When the drops get to your feet, allow them to flow off the tip of your toes and sink down into the earth. Follow the water with your attention and feel yourself being connected energetically to the center of the earth. Pause there and take several slow, deep breaths.

8. When you're ready, imagine scooping up the second bucket of water from the same source and repeating the process for the back of your body.

9. The third bucket is for the sides of your body, so the drop splits as soon as it touches the top of your head. Again, after the drops flow off the sides of your feet into the earth, spend as much time as you like imagining yourself connected energetically to the center of the earth and breathing slowly and deeply.

10. When you're ready, bring your attention to the touch of your body on the seat, take one last deep breath in and open your eyes.

When first learning this meditation, you may want to use physical touch to get your attention started on the right path. With your eyes still closed, you can lightly touch the top of your head with your finger to help trigger the tingly feeling of the water. Then, with your finger, continue to trace the path of the water along your skin as far as your hands can reach without bending over. After practicing for a while, you may want to stop using the touching technique because you can feel the tingling of the water without it. Even though I typically don't trace the water with my finger now, I add back this helpful technique on days when my mind is especially tenacious about not giving up the talking stick. As a general rule, I also add it back if it is the third time in a row that I have started a bucket over again because my mind chatter budged in before the water made it past my big nose.

The feeling you get when imagining the water touching your skin may be different than mine, and may change on different days. Master Fu taught me that if you feel "something," that is probably it. For me, it feels like a little electric tingle. A friend of mine says that it feels like the light touch of a feather or a paint brush.

It may take a little practice, but the vibes will come. Master Fu anticipated, correctly, that I might doubt that the feelings I was feeling were more than "just my imagination" and therefore powerless. So, he offered a self-test, called "The Hot Hand Test" that can be used to verify that you are "getting it." (I've included it at the end of the book.)

# *Advanced Dumping Buckets techniques*

Once you're comfortable with the basic technique outlined above, feel free to alter the meditation in any way you like. Here are few alterations that I recommend giving a try:

- **Standing Dumping Buckets:** Follow the basic steps while standing with a relaxed posture. Keep your torso straight and bend your knees slightly (though not so far that you need to use a lot of strength in your legs).
- **Sheets of Water:** Gradually let more water spill out from the buckets so that you eventually feel a sheet of water flowing over the whole surface of your body.
- **Deep Tissue Buckets:** Let the tingling of the water sink past the surface of your skin into your tissue and bones as it is traveling, particularly at spots that seem to be calling out for a little extra dose.
- **Walking With Buckets:** Dump buckets with your eyes open while you are doing something that doesn't require thinking. When I do this while I am walking, I like to stagger the speed of the drops when they reach my ankles so that each rolls off when their respective foot is planted.

## *Standing in a slow grocery store checkout line*

My key take-home message from this chapter is that any place could be a place to experience spiritual vibes. I was recently waiting in line to pay for some groceries. I had been nudging my shopping cart forward in the line for a good amount of time when a second cashier popped up from behind and said: "I can take care of you over here." Before I had even had time to turn my head to see the speaker, the woman behind me in line had barreled her stuffed cart over to the newly opened checkout stand. I wanted to protest but she had already started unloading her shopping. The voices in my head jumped into uproar. One voice in my head was scolding my rival customer: "That's not fair!" Another was scolding the cashier. A third was lecturing an imaginary manager at the store on how to train the cashiers to treat their customers better. A fourth voice tried to dampen the clamour by accusing the others of being petty. He pointed out that they didn't know what was going on in the rival customer's life and that she might have a good reason for her seemingly selfish act. Then the four of them started a running commentary, like a panel of experts watching a sporting event, as my eyes scrutinized her appearance for any indication that she was facing some dire situation that justified her stealing time away from me.

Thankfully, at this point, I recognized that I was feeling and probably radiating very negative vibes and looked for the source. I realized that a futile war zone had erupted in my thought world and I called for the "bucket cavalry." I closed my eyes and did a quick standing version of Dumping Buckets. This had the effect of shutting off my inner voices for a split second and I had a flash of feeling interconnected with everybody and everything in the store. In that moment, all that useless strife was washed away into a sea of compassion.

# SUMMARY

- Both religious and non-religious spaces can have spiritual vibes and engender a sense of connection with the divine or sacred.
- Emotion traces or residue may be a cause of such vibes, and there is some evidence that acoustic effects could be contributing factors in some auspicious venues.
- Meditation is a vital method to move us out of "thinking" and quiet the mind in order to take us into a place where we are able to feel less a specific individual and more a part of and open to the vibrations around us.
- The take-home message from this chapter is that any place could be a place to experience spiritual vibes.

# CHAPTER 8

## VIBING WITH NATURE

I got to chatting with a park ranger at the Muir Woods National Monument in California and they confided in me that it is not unheard of for couples to meander off to secluded spots in the forest to get immersed in nature together – so to speak. He was convinced that something about the towering redwood trees seems to inspire their impishness. I don't know if that is the case but I can certainly attest to getting a deep forest vibe there that is profoundly moving. I recommend visiting this old-growth redwood forest to anyone as an opportunity to experience the awe of some of nature's most majestic creations without having to gear up for a strenuous hike. Do what you will with your awe.

This chapter explores the vibes that people get when interacting with phenomena of the natural world as it is, including the earth and plants. Nature is a uniquely powerful source of vibes. To quote John Muir, the naturalist known as the Father of National Parks: "The clearest way into the universe is through a forest wilderness." My experience is also that spending time in forests, and engaging with nature in general, is a highly effective way to dissolve away the illusion of separateness. Nature is also a source of beneficial biophysical vibes, like the earth's natural electric charge that is believed to stabilize the electricity of the body, and of nurturing subconscious vibes stemming from humanity's historical connection with the natural world – nearly our entire evolutionary process unfolded with us immersed in nature.

In this chapter, I'll describe two simple and gentle practices for "tuning in" to the earth – Earthing and forest bathing. I'll also discuss psychedelic mushrooms and provide brief highlights of the health-related research that has been conducted with these, along with general guidelines for approaching the endeavor and helpful resources.

## *Earthing*

Some people love to shed their shoes whenever possible to let their feet breathe while others are content to have their feet bundled up in footwear most of the time. One of the few studies of barefoot behavior found a positive association between going barefoot outside and feeling connected to nature, as measured by the connectedness to nature scale

(Harvey, et al., 2016). Participants filled out questionnaires asking about their barefoot preferences under different conditions and related behaviors, beliefs and feelings associated with going barefoot, especially outdoors. The results showed that going barefoot outside helped them to feel more relaxed and enhanced their feeling of nature immersion. Taking it a step further, there have been numerous research articles and books published recently that tout various health benefits associated with "earthing," which refers to the practice of maintaining an electrical connection between the human body and the ground through touch.

Earthing is typically accomplished through outdoor activities like walking barefoot on the beach and gardening with bare hands, or even indoors using an earthing device by connecting wires to furniture, like your bed, to transfer the Earth's electrons from the ground into the body. The bed-earthing devices consist of a special fitted sheet connected to a wire that you connect to the grounding hole of a grounded electrical outlet. You are meant to sleep on the special sheet naked. This grounding hole is connected to a wire that provides a safe path for any dangerous electrical current to pass into the ground under the house. The bed-earthing devices take advantage of this path to allow the Earth's electrons to go the other way. If you do not have grounded electrical outlets or prefer not to use the outlet, there are other earthing devices that consist of a rod that you drive into the ground next to your house and connect to the special sheet with a long wire.

The theory behind the practice is that bodily contact with the Earth's natural electric charge stabilizes the electricity of the body. While there are reports that earthing promotes a host of beneficial physiological changes and reported wellbeing (Chevalier, et al., 2012), there is no consensus among researchers from an electrical perspective regarding whether enough electrons flow between the human body and the earth to mediate these effects. One study using sensitive instrumentation was able to show electrical current flow between human subjects and the ground under some conditions at the range of 0.000000001 amperes (Chamberlin, et al., 2014). This level of current flow is in the ballpark of the tiny currents picked up by the antennae of cellular phones, which theoretically could be enough to impact our health over the long run. Future research will sort that out.

## *Earthing was the "norm" for 99.99% of human evolution*

What is more interesting to me is the possibility that subconscious vibes might be involved because our bodies are craving contact with nature.

Modern lifestyles separate humans from exposure to nature to a degree that is unnatural relative to the way that we evolved. Premodern humans were almost always going about their days immersed in nature, and in contact with the ground. We have evolved that way for around 7 million years and only in the last 0.01% of that time have we started to insulate our bodies from it with synthetic materials in the soles of our shoes (leather-soled shoes don't count). Likewise, insulating materials in our domiciles were not a thing while virtually all of our DNA adaptation molding took place. Considering this very recent and very drastic switch, it seems plausible that we modern humans feel a bit deprived of earth contact at a subconscious level, and this is the source of at least some of the good vibes that people feel in nature.

Vibes and DNA aside, social scientists have looked into why people feel good vibes in nature for practical purposes. Pertinent to urban planning, for example, a study published in the *International Journal of Environmental Health Research* found that spending time in an urban park can have a positive impact on a person's sense of wellbeing and this impact was strongest if the time spent in the park was at least 20 minutes (Yuen and Jenkins, 2020). A fascinating social science experiment that brought to mind the Muir Woods story involved analyzing people's responses to viewing a towering tree for one minute compared to their responses viewing a building of the same height. The results showed that those looking at the tree reported stronger feelings of awe, and also that their "awe scores" were associated with more pro-social helping behaviors, such as generosity and enhanced collective concern (Piff, et al., 2015).

The most impactful example of research on nature vibes for me is the study showing evidence that a 90-minute walk in nature can reduce the activity of the part of the brain that is associated with rumination. Rumination is one of the scientific terms for what I see as getting stuck in the "thinking world." The researchers defined rumination as negative repetitive thoughts, linking with mental health problems. The part of the brain they monitored was located in a subdivision of the area called the prefrontal cortex, often called the PFC. They were interested in that brain area because activity in that spot had previously been linked to rumination in both depressed and healthy people. The results of the nature walk experiment were that this brief activity in nature decreased both self-reported rumination and brain activity in that part of the PFC, whereas a city walk did not (Bratman, et al., 2015).

# Immersion in nature is still an option

Forest Bathing, or Shinrin-yoku, is a formalized form of nature walk. This excellent method of getting a dose of nature immersion originated in Japan and is gaining popularity across the globe. The essence of the method is to maintain your attention in the present moment while you are appreciating nature. The most basic instruction for forest bathing is to go to a forest and wander around aimlessly, paying attention with all of your senses. Here is an expanded version:

1. Go to a forest or any place where you are surrounded by nature.
2. Go untethered. Leave your cell phone at home. Don't take a camera or other distractions. Leave your goals at home too.
3. Allow yourself to wander while softly gazing, smelling, listening and "tuning in" to the vibes of nature, however they may come to you.
4. Pause from time to time to see if your body feels pulled in any particular direction.
5. As you feel like it, sit for a while and be still. Observe how the behavior of the birds and other forest life changes as they become accustomed to your presence.

6. If you go with others, make an agreement to refrain from conversation. You can gather at the end of your walk and share your stories.
7. In the hours after you complete your walk, notice any lasting effects.

I neglected to mention above that walking around outside barefoot is not risk-free. One sad statistic that drives this point home was found in a study of in-patients with diabetic foot ulcers. The finding was that nearly half of the ulcers resulted from accidentally stepping on sharp objects with bare feet (Gale, et al., 2008). Therefore, it is important to only walk barefoot when it is safe and practical. Regarding forest bathing, safety tips include:

1. Wear appropriate footwear.
2. Always pay attention to your surroundings.
3. If the terrain is dangerous, stay on marked trails.
4. Remember to consider things like sun protection and allergies.
5. Avoid touching any leaves unless you are sure they are not poisonous.
6. Bring a friend or let someone know where you're going and for how long.

A recent review of research evaluating the health-related impact of forest bathing concluded that there is strong evidence that it can be effective in improving mental health, especially reducing anxiety (Kotera, et al., 2022). There is also preliminary evidence suggesting that forest bathing can have positive effects on the body's physiology. One example that I find particularly compelling is a study looking at natural killer cells. These cells are important players in the body's immune system. They get rid of bad cells that could cause problems, like cells infected with viruses. The results showed that a three-day forest bathing workshop increased the number and activity of natural killer cells compared with three days of walking in a city (Li, 2010). You can find forest bathing workshops offered at retreat centers all around the world.

## Nature's superconscious vibe inducers

Now I want to talk about a potent, forest-derived aid for tapping into superconsious vibes. Mushrooms are Earth's principal source of psychedelics – naturally occurring chemicals that are powerful inducers of altered states of consciousness (Lowe, et al., 2021). The chemicals interact with neurotransmitter receptors in our nervous system (e.g., serotonin receptors) to shift the information signaling pathways (or brain functional connectivity) in a way that tamps down the sense of the self as an isolated entity. A leading theory for how this shift occurs is that there is a temporary slowing of activity in the part of the brain where the self talks to itself, called the default mode network (Preller, et al., 2020). Similar shifts have been reported in studies of long-term meditators (e.g., Buddhist monks) and are considered crucial for the transition from "normal" states of consciousness to meditative states (Marzetti, et al., 2014; Raffone, et al., 2019). Essentially, psychedelics are a catalyst to accessing a state of consciousness where the self is experienced as fundamentally related or interconnected with all that is.

Humans have harnessed this power throughout history, often as part of religious and spiritual ceremonies. This is why another term used for psychedelics is entheogen, which comes from Greek terms to convey the meaning "generating or creating the divine within."

Psilocybin is a psychedelic chemical found in a family of gilled mushrooms commonly called "magic mushrooms." It was first isolated in the 1950s and initial research on psilocybin and other psychedelics indicated the potential for their use in the treatment of neuropsychiatric conditions. The US government put a stop to scientific research on psychedelics in 1970, as a result of politics and prankstering, but now research in this area has been revived. A study pivotal to this revival was conducted in 2004 by researchers from the University of California, Los Angeles, who explored the potential of psilocybin treatment in patients with advanced-stage cancer (Grob, et al., 2011). The UCLA group demonstrated that psilocybin can be used safely with cancer patients and may also be beneficial at reducing depression and anxiety associated with psychological crises due to a terminal diagnosis. Since then, scientists researching psychedelics have been on a roll.

Key recent findings related to magic mushrooms include a string of preliminary studies showing evidence of an antidepressant effect of psilocybin-assisted therapy, followed by a blockbuster confirmatory study conducted at Johns Hopkins Bayview Medical Center in Baltimore, Maryland, and published in one of the most prestigious American medical journals. The preliminary studies evaluated depression among patients with life-threatening cancer and patients with treatment-resistant depression (Griffiths, et al., 2016; Ross, et al., 2016; Carhart-Harris, et al., 2016). The confirmatory study was a randomized clinical trial of 24 participants with major depressive disorder published in the *Journal of the American Medical*

*Association* (JAMA Psychiatry) in 2021 (Davis, et al., 2021). The term "randomized clinical trial" tells you that the study followed the gold standard of control conditions required for testing new pharmaceutical drugs and other medical treatments. The results of the JAMA study showed that two psilocybin-assisted therapy sessions were sufficient to produce rapid and large antidepressant effects in patients with major depressive disorder, and these improvements were sustained for at least a month.

## *How to "shroom" without being in a research study*

Phonetically speaking, there are three "S"s to keep in mind if you are interested in embarking on a therapeutic "trip" with magic mushrooms outside a research lab: psychological support, set and setting:

1. **Psychological support** means another human by your side throughout the approximately eight-hour experience. This is important both to keep you safe and to be sure that you feel safe (more on this "S" in the next section).
2. **Set** refers to your mindset. This, along with #3, are fundamental concepts in the field of psychedelic research established in the early 1960s (Leary,

et al., 1963). Having a positive mindset at the initiation of the experience is critical for launching the trip in a positive direction. It is also advisable to be mentally prepared for your thinking mind to let go of its typical controlling mode. A recent study found that having "clear intentions" for the experience was conducive to mystical-type experiences (Haijen, et al., 2018).

3. **Setting** refers to the place you're in during the trip. Being in a safe place is paramount and, as with #1, this applies to both the actual physical environment and the individual's feelings of safety.

Set and setting are factors that are highly individualized and specific to a given moment in one's life. You will know best how to arrange these. Psychological support, on the other hand, relies on another human to act as your guide on the trip. Michael Pollan is an Emeritus Professor of the University of California, Berkeley Graduate School of Journalism who has provided a frank and comprehensive description of how all this works in his book, *How to Change Your Mind* (Pollan, 2018). Pollan recounts his experiences as a late—blooming psychonaut, a term referring to someone who explores altered states of consciousness using psychedelics, which he began doing in his fifties, and not without trepidation. I highly recommend this book to anybody considering becoming a psychonaut, regardless of your age.

## *Psychological support centers*

You can find integrative healthcare clinics that are "psychedelic-friendly," meaning that they will provide a supportive environment where, without judgement, you can find meaning in psychedelic experiences. An example of this is Sage Integrative Health in Berkeley, California, which hosts a regular psychedelic integration circle at their clinic.

A typical protocol you might expect when working with a plant medicine guide would likely involve many or all of the following steps:

1. Meet for a pre-trip orientation session.
2. As homework before your trip session, complete an autobiography worksheet to give your guide a deep understanding of you, your intentions for the trip and any personal issues that you might expect to face during the trip.
3. Show up with your magic mushrooms in hand. Since it is illegal in most parts of the world to possess, sell or transport psilocybin mushrooms, your guide will expect you to somehow legally obtain your shrooms.

4. Meet afterwards to support processing of the experience.

Synthesis is a retreat center in Amsterdam that gets around the legal issues with psilocybin mushrooms by offering an alternative source of psilocybin: magic truffles. These are the root-like structures of the magic mushrooms that also contain psilocybin but are not illegal. Professional facilitators at Synthesis lead psychonauts on journeys to awaken expanded forms of consciousness, through ceremony, open-dialogue, bodywork, meditation, sound and psychedelic education.

## Be sure to mitigate risks

I want to provide the caution that there are risks associated with psilocybin and other psychedelics. Most importantly, some people who are vulnerable or disposed to serious forms of mental illness, like schizophrenia, can be triggered into their first psychotic break by a bad psychedelic trip. You should always consult your physician/doctor if you are considering becoming a psychonaut.

## *Catalysts for consciousness change*

I'll leave those important words of caution as my parting thoughts for this chapter and end with a quote by Albert Hofmann, the chemist that first identified and synthesized the psychoactive compounds in magic mushrooms. The following excerpt from a letter he wrote in 2007 strikes me as an eloquent way to tie together the themes we've covered.

*"Alienation from nature and the loss of the experience of being part of the living creation is the greatest tragedy of our materialistic era. It is the causative reason for ecological devastation and climate change. Therefore, I attribute the absolute highest importance to consciousness change. I regard psychedelics as catalyzers for this. They are tools which are guiding our perception toward other deeper areas of our human existence, so that we again become aware of our spiritual essence. Psychedelic experiences in a safe setting can help our consciousness open up to this sensation of connection and of being one with nature."*
*– Albert Hofmann*

# SUMMARY

- Nature is a powerful source of beneficial biophysical vibes and nearly all of our evolutionary process unfolded with nature as a greater part of our daily lives.
- Earthing and forest bathing are accessible practical methods to engage with nature and dissolve away the illusion of separateness from nature. Preliminary research shows that forest bathing can also have beneficial effects on the body's physiology, bolstering the body's immune system.
- Magic mushrooms can open the door to experiencing superconscious vibes (deep interconnectedness with the world).
- Research has shown that psilocybin-assisted therapy treatment has a distinct short- and long-term antidepressant effect for patients with major depressive disorder.

# FINAL WORDS

In this little book, we've taken a modern, scientific look at vibes in all forms. By focusing on information gained through current scientific methods, I do not mean to discount esoteric knowledge passed down through mystical traditions. Both of these ways of knowing are valuable and often produce strikingly similar results. For example, Hermeticism is a branch of spiritual philosophy dating back as early as the first century AD (Alfonso-Goldfarb and Jubran, 2008) and one of its primary principles, and an often cited "Universal Law" of the world, is – "Nothing rests; everything moves; everything vibrates" – conveying essentially the same meaning as the quote by physicist Max Plank that began the book: "All the physical matters are composed of vibration."

And it's not just mystics and scientists touting the importance of vibes. One of the first self-help books published in the US, *Think and Grow Rich* by Napoleon Hill, was based on the author interviewing 500 people in business who had amassed personal fortunes – to find out what they had done to attain their success – and one of the major conclusions of the book is: ". . . we are what we are because of the vibrations of thought which we pick up and register, . . ." (Hill, 2005). Originally published in 1937, Hill's book is considered a classic in the personal development genre and, despite the title's emphasis on increasing income, the ideas presented are essentially a twentieth-century interpretation of what are called the Universal Laws attributed to hermetic philosophy. Arguably, the most fundamental of these natural laws is the Universal Law of Vibration, which states: *"The universe responds to your vibration. It will return whatever energy you put out."* (King, 2018.)

According to the Universal Law of Vibration, humans are transmitters and receivers of vibrational frequencies and the vibrations we put out are constantly pulling in stuff that's vibrating at a similar frequency to us. The concept that we are "transmitters and receivers of vibrational frequencies" jives with the science we have reviewed in this book. For example, studies described in the first chapter explored how the biophysical vibes shown to be emitted from our hearts, in the form of EMFs, are able to transfer energy to that of another person. The "pulling in" half of this natural law – that the vibrations we put out are constantly pulling in stuff vibrating at a similar frequency to us – is far less studied. The best example that I know of is an experiment conducted at Stanford University studying a Loving-Kindness Meditation directing well-wishing to foster a feeling of selfless love. The Stanford group found that a brief loving-kindness exercise increases feelings of social connectedness and may help to decrease social isolation (Hutcherson, et al., 2008). I consider this strong supporting evidence for the principle because putting out selfless love vibes and "pulling in" increased social connectedness seems like a pretty good match in terms of vibrational frequencies.

As to why vibes matter, we've reviewed various ways in which we talk about vibing with those around us or feeling vibes in places and, in most cases, there is science to back it up. For example, the "neural coupling" revealed by brain scans that connects storytellers and listeners as the listener's brain activity mimics that of the person telling the story is a likely biophysical basis for the feeling that you're "on the same wavelength" as someone. We've also seen that we are essentially swimming in a sea of invisible vibes that we're not consciously aware of but have significant impact on the choices we make, how we feel, and even our health. Color can account for 90% of snap judgments made about products, clutter in a home is correlated with life dissatisfaction, and twenty minutes of soaking in nature vibes has a measurable, positive impact on a person's sense of wellbeing, among other examples. Some of the vibes that affect our lives the most are even more hidden from our perception. Biophysical vibes triggered by odorless chemicals released from a woman's tears can squelch men's libido levels, for example, and even result in a dip in testosterone levels in their blood and decreased brain activity in the parts of the brain associated with sexual arousal. More generally, our emotional state is reflected in patterns in our EMF spreading vibes to those around us. Research has shown that these vibes can result in energy transfer between the EMFs of two people in close proximity. So, our vibe (be it positive or negative) can be subconsciously picked up on and physically absorbed by others, and vice versa – which ought to give you an incentive to try your best to maintain a positive attitude and to spend as much time as possible surrounded by positive people.

Based on the agreements between spiritual philosophies and modern science we've discussed, by improving our awareness of the vibes around us and of how they influence our behaviors and relationships, and by raising our vibrational frequencies and sending out love vibes, we will experience more positive actions and love in our life and contribute to manifesting a more peaceful and co-operative society. There are also practical ways in which our understanding of the wealth of subconscious vibes can help us – from alerting us to imperceptible dangers in our environment or people who are good "friend material" to loftier reasons such as the ability of superconscious vibes to temporarily break the illusion of our separateness and carry us to states of mind where individuality itself seems to dissolve into the "real world."

This book has given you a behind-the-scenes knowledge of vibes and some simple tools for harnessing them. It's time for you now to explore your experience of vibes more deeply and unlock the mysteries of how our minds influence the physical world and how we can transcend the limitations of space and time. Bon voyage!

# THE HOT HAND TEST

To start this test, you need a helper and a pen.

1. Begin by pressing your palms together in front of your face and lining up the tips of your middle fingers so that they are exactly even. Keeping your palms pressed together with the tips of the middle fingers at exactly the same height, ask your helper to draw a line across the base of your hands, just above your wrists where the fleshy parts of your two thumbs meet. This mark across the base of both of your hands will allow you to line your hands up later in the same position – by lining up the pen mark. This concludes the "pre" part of the test, and now your helper can stay or go.

2. Next, close your eyes and do a meditation practice of your choice to tune in to your energy or a few minutes of the slow-breathing practice described in Chapter 1. Once you've started to feel like you've tuned in to your energy – however that feels to you – begin the "hot hand" part of the test.

3. In your mind's eye, see one of your hands start to glow with heat. Imagine your energy flowing like lava down your arm and filling up your hand. Feel your hand pulsing with the intense heat. Imagine it is red hot, blue hot, violet hot . . . whatever you can imagine about searing heat.

4. After about a minute of this visualization, open your eyes for the "post" part of the test. Bring your palms together with the pen mark lining up straight across both thumb pads and see if the tip of your hot hand's middle finger is now taller than its partner. If your fingers still line up evenly, return to your meditation practice, see if you can go deeper into it, and then repeat the post test.

You can repeat this cycle as many times as it takes to see a difference in the height of your fingers. When the tip of your hot hand's middle finger does get taller than its partner, you have your objective verification. Feel free to revel for a moment in the magnificence of your ability to influence your physical body with your imagination.

The Hot Hand Test isn't hard-wired into our genes. The esoteric explanation for how you can make your hand bigger with your mind is conveyed in the principle found in Traditional Chinese Medicine: Yi Dao Qi Tao. This can be translated literally as "Thought arrives, qi arrives," and means roughly: "Where thought goes, qi follows."

According to this principle, the Hot Hand Test results shows that subtle energy qi follows your attention to make your hand swell. The strictly by-the-biology-book explanation is that your hand swells because of increased blood flow to the tiny blood vessels that end in your hand tissue, but what triggered the increased blood flow to one hand and not the other is a mystery.

What is *not* a mystery in all of the biology books is that increased blood flow to our tissues is almost always a very good thing. In fact, increased peripheral microcirculation (as it is called in the books) is often touted as a mechanism underlying the restorative properties and health benefits of meditation in general (Ravinder, et al., 2014). This makes a lot of sense from the medical point of view because:

1. Tissues need blood flow to stay healthy. Blood flow brings nutrients to every cell in every tissue and carries away the stuff to be recycled. If you slow that flow, you diminish the vitality of the cells and of the tissues, and that can lead to disease. Doctors will back this statement up with a mountain of facts, including that decreased peripheral microcirculation is an early hallmark of several cardiovascular and metabolic diseases.

Even years before a disease is detected in an organ, they can see decreased blood flow.

2. Meditation activates the body's parasympathetic nervous system, which turns on the "chill vibe," which increases peripheral microcirculation throughout the body. The increase is due to hormones and other neurotransmitters that increase the diameter of the tiny blood vessels reaching into every nook and cranny of all of our tissues.

The beauty of this medical perspective is that you don't have to believe in any of the qi/subtle energy/crystal-chakra stuff, or any sort of hocus-pocus to experience the benefits of paying attention to your vibes. You can literally improve your health by simply "chilling" once in a while. And the more often, the better. You don't even have to do this by meditating. You can activate your parasympathetic nervous system by engaging in any activity that relaxes you, like exercising, getting a massage, playing music or wrestling with your pet.

# ACKNOWLEDGEMENTS

My appreciation to the lovely champion for the inner psychic in all of us, Theresa Cheung, who coaxed this book into existence and introduced me to my brilliant publisher at Welbeck, Jo Lal, and my gifted editor, Kate Latham, who both made the book you have read intelligible, and who were a joy to work with.

Deepest thanks to my colleagues at the Institute of Noetic Sciences (IONS), especially Stanley Krippner, Marilyn Schlitz, Elizabeth Targ, and Cassandra Vieten who coaxed me on board, and to all the supporters of IONS who make our consciousness research possible.

# REFERENCES

## Introduction and Chapter 1

Baldwin, A. L., Rand, W. L., and Schwartz, G. E. (2013). Practicing Reiki does not appear to routinely produce high-intensity electromagnetic fields from the heart or hands of Reiki practitioners. *Journal of Alternative and Complementary Medicine (New York, N.Y.)*, *19*(6), 518–526. https://doi.org/10.1089/acm.2012.0136

Cohen, D., Palti, Y., Cuffin, B. N., and Schmid, S. J. (1980). Magnetic fields produced by steady currents in the body. *Proceedings of the National Academy of Sciences of the United States of America*, *77*(3), 1447–1451. https://doi.org/10.1073/pnas.77.3.1447

Gelstein, S., Yeshurun, Y., Rozenkrantz, L., Shushan, S., Frumin, I., Roth, Y., and Sobel, N. (2011). Human tears contain a chemosignal. *Science (New York, N.Y.)*, *331*(6014), 226–230. https://doi.org/10.1126/science.1198331

Greenwald, A. G., Poehlman, T. A., Uhlmann, E. L., and Banaji, M. R. (2009). Understanding and Using the Implicit Association Test: III. Meta-analysis of predictive validity. *Journal of Personality and Social Psychology*, *97*(1), 17–41. https://doi.org/10.1037/a0015575

Haidt, J. (2013). *The Righteous Mind: Why Good People Are Divided by Politics and Religion*. Knopf Doubleday Publishing Group.

Jacob, T.J.C., Wang, L., Jaffer, S., McPhee, S. (2006). Changes in the Odor Quality of Androstadienone During Exposure-Induced Sensitization. *Chemical Senses*, 31(1), 3–8. https://doi.org/10.1093/chemse/bji073

Jayawardena, R., Ranasinghe, P., Ranawaka, H., Gamage, N., Dissanayake, D., and Misra, A. (2020). Exploring the Therapeutic Benefits of Pranayama (Yogic Breathing): A Systematic Review. *International Journal of Yoga*, *13*(2), 99–110. https://doi.org/10.4103/ijoy.IJOY_37_19

Kennedy, J. M., and Brown, K. (1970). Effects of male odor during infancy on the maturation, behavior and reproduction of female mice. *Developmental Psychobiology*, *3*(3), 179–189. https://doi.org/10.1002/dev.420030305

Lufityanto, G., Donkin, C., and Pearson, J. (2016). Measuring Intuition: Nonconscious Emotional Information Boosts Decision Accuracy and Confidence. *Psychological Science*, *27*(5), 622–634. https://doi.org/10.1177/0956797616629403

McCraty, R. (2003). The Energetic Heart: Bioelectromagnetic Interactions Within and Between People. *The Neuropsychotherapist*, *6*, 22–43. https://doi.org/10.12744/tnpt(6)022-043

Murphy, M. R. (1973). Effects of female hamster vaginal discharge on the behavior of male hamsters. *Behavioral Biology*, *9*(3), 367–375. https://doi.org/10.1016/s0091-6773(73)80185-3

Muscatell, K. A., and Eisenberger, N. I. (2012). A Social Neuroscience Perspective on Stress and Health. *Social and Personality Psychology Compass*, *6*(12), 890–904. https://doi.org/10.1111/j.1751-9004.2012.00467.x

Pal, G. K., Velkumary, S., and Madanmohan. (2004). Effect of short-term practice of breathing exercises on autonomic functions in normal human volunteers. *Indian J Med Res*, *120*(2), 115–121.

Pramanik, T., Sharma, H. O., Mishra, S., Mishra, A., Prajapati, R., and Singh, S. (2009). Immediate effect of slow pace bhastrika pranayama on blood pressure and heart rate. *Journal of Alternative and Complementary Medicine (New York, N.Y.)*, *15*(3), 293–295. https://doi.org/10.1089/acm.2008.0440

Ravreby, I., Snitz, K., and Sobel, N. (2022). There is chemistry in social chemistry. *Science Advances*, *8*(25), eabn0154. https://doi.org/10.1126/sciadv.abn0154

Rubik, B., Muehsam, D., Hammerschlag, R., and Jain, S. (2015). Biofield science and healing: History, terminology, and concepts. *Global Advances in Health and Medicine*, *4*(1_suppl), gahmj-2015.

Russo, M. A., Santarelli, D. M., and O'Rourke, D. (2017). The physiological effects of slow breathing in the healthy human. *Breathe (Sheffield, England)*, *13*(4), 298–309. https://doi.org/10.1183/20734735.009817

Saxton, T. K., Lyndon, A., Little, A. C., and Roberts, S. C. (2008). Evidence that androstadienone, a putative human chemosignal, modulates women's attributions of men's attractiveness. *Hormones and Behavior*, *54*(5), 597–601. https://doi.org/10.1016/j.yhbeh.2008.06.001

Tsunoda, M., Miyamichi, K., Eguchi, R., Sakuma, Y., Yoshihara, Y., Kikusui, T., Kuwahara, M., and Touhara, K. (2018). Identification of an Intra- and Inter-specific Tear Protein Signal in Rodents. *Current Biology: CB*, *28*(8), 1213–1223. e6. https://doi.org/10.1016/j.cub.2018.02.060

Wyatt, T. D. (2015). The search for human pheromones: The lost decades and the necessity of returning to first principles. *Proceedings. Biological Sciences, 282*(1804), 20142994. https://doi.org/10.1098/rspb.2014.2994

Zulfiqar, U., Jurivich, D. A., Gao, W., and Singer, D. H. (2010). Relation of high heart rate variability to healthy longevity. *The American Journal of Cardiology, 105*(8), 1181–1185. https://doi.org/10.1016/j.amjcard.2009.12.022

## Chapter 2

Becker, A. J., Uckert, S., Stief, C. G., Scheller, F., Knapp, W. H., Hartmann, U., Brabant, G., and Jonas, U. (2002). Serum levels of human growth hormone during different penile conditions in the cavernous and systemic blood of healthy men and patients with erectile dysfunction. *Urology, 59*(4), 609–614. https://doi.org/10.1016/s0090-4295(01)01594-1

Becker, A. J., Uckert, S., Stief, C. G., Truss, M. C., Machtens, S., Scheller, F., Knapp, W. H., Hartmann, U., and Jonas, U. (2000). Possible role of human growth hormone in penile erection. *The Journal of Urology, 164*(6), 2138–2142.

Carrellas, B., and Sprinkle, A. (2007). *Urban Tantra: Sacred Sex for the Twenty-First Century*. Celestial Arts.

Cera, N., Vargas-Cáceres, S., Oliveira, C., Monteiro, J., Branco, D., Pignatelli, D., and Rebelo, S. (2021). How Relevant is the Systemic Oxytocin Concentration for Human Sexual Behavior? A Systematic Review. *Sexual Medicine. 9*(4): 100370. doi: 10.1016/j.esxm.2021.100370.

# REFERENCES

Corradini, A., and Antonietti, A. (2013). Mirror neurons and their function in cognitively understood empathy. *Consciousness and Cognition, 22*(3), 1152–1161. https://doi.org/10.1016/j.concog.2013.03.003

Emmons, R. A., and McCullough, M. E. (2003). Counting blessings versus burdens: An experimental investigation of gratitude and subjective wellbeing in daily life. *Journal of Personality and Social Psychology, 84*(2), 377–389. https://doi.org/10.1037//0022-3514.84.2.377

Feldman, R. (2012). Oxytocin and social affiliation in humans. *Hormones and Behavior, 61*(3), 380–391. https://doi.org/10.1016/j.yhbeh.2012.01.008

Fisher, H., Aron, A., and Brown, L. L. (2005). Romantic love: An fMRI study of a neural mechanism for mate choice. *The Journal of Comparative Neurology, 493*(1), 58–62. https://doi.org/10.1002/cne.20772

Galdiero, M., Pivonello, R., Grasso, L. F. S., Cozzolino, A., and Colao, A. (2012). Growth hormone, prolactin, and sexuality. *Journal of Endocrinological Investigation, 35*(8), 782–794. https://doi.org/10.1007/BF03345805

Gallese, V., Fadiga, L., Fogassi, L., and Rizzolatti, G. (1996). Action recognition in the premotor cortex. *Brain: A Journal of Neurology, 119 (Pt 2),* 593–609. https://doi.org/10.1093/brain/119.2.593

Kenkel, W. M., Paredes, J., Yee, J. R., Pournajafi-Nazarloo, H., Bales, K. L., and Carter, C. S. (2012). Neuroendocrine and behavioral responses to exposure to an infant in male prairie voles. *Journal of Neuroendocrinology, 24*(6), 874–886. https://doi.org/10.1111/j.1365-2826.2012.02301.x

Liu, L., Zhang, Y., Zhou, Q., Garrett, D. D., Lu, C., Chen, A., Qiu, J., and Ding, G. (2020). Auditory–Articulatory Neural Alignment between Listener and Speaker during Verbal Communication. *Cerebral Cortex*, *30*(3), 942–951. https://doi.org/10.1093/cercor/bhz138

Motofei, I. G., and Rowland, D. L. (2005). The physiological basis of human sexual arousal: Neuroendocrine sexual asymmetry. *International Journal of Andrology*, *28*(2), 78–87. https://doi.org/10.1111/j.1365-2605.2004.00514.x

Seligman, M. E. P., Steen, T. A., Park, N., and Peterson, C. (2005). Positive psychology progress: Empirical validation of interventions. *The American Psychologist*, *60*(5), 410–421. https://doi.org/10.1037/0003-066X.60.5.410

Stephens, G. J., Silbert, L. J., and Hasson, U. (2010). Speaker-listener neural coupling underlies successful communication. *Proceedings of the National Academy of Sciences of the United States of America*, *107*(32), 14425–14430. https://doi.org/10.1073/pnas.1008662107

Wood, A. M., Joseph, S., Lloyd, J., and Atkins, S. (2009). Gratitude influences sleep through the mechanism of pre-sleep cognitions. *Journal of Psychosomatic Research*, *66*(1), 43–48. https://doi.org/10.1016/j.jpsychores.2008.09.002

## Chapter 3

Brabant, O. (2016). More Than Meets the Eye: Toward a Post-Materialist Model of Consciousness. *Explore (New York, N.Y.)*, *12*(5), 347–354. https://doi.org/10.1016/j.explore.2016.06.006

Cap, A. (2011). *Beyond Goodbye: An Extraordinary Story of a Shared Death Experience*. Paragon Publishing.

# REFERENCES

Church, D., Stapleton, P., Mollon, P., Feinstein, D., Boath, E., Mackay, D., and Sims, R. (2018a). Guidelines for the Treatment of PTSD Using Clinical EFT (Emotional Freedom Techniques). *Healthcare (Basel, Switzerland)*, 6(4), 146. https://doi.org/10.3390/healthcare6040146

Church, D., Yount, G., and Brooks, A. J. (2012). The effect of Emotional Freedom Techniques on stress biochemistry: A randomized controlled trial. *The Journal of Nervous and Mental Disease*, 200(10), 891–896.

Church, D., Yount, G., Rachlin, K., Fox, L., and Nelms, J. (2018b). Epigenetic Effects of PTSD Remediation in Veterans Using Clinical Emotional Freedom Techniques: A Randomized Controlled Pilot Study. *American Journal of Health Promotion*, 32(1), 112–122.

Lane, J. (2009). The Neurochemistry of Counterconditioning: Acupressure Desensitization in Psychotherapy. *Energy Psychology Journal*, 1(1), 31–44. https://doi.org/10.9769/EPJ.2009.1.1.JRL

Mayer, E. L. (2002). Freud and Jung: The boundaried mind and the radically connected mind. *The Journal of Analytical Psychology*, 47(1), 91–99. https://doi.org/10.1111/1465-5922.00291

Yogananda, P. (1994). *Autobiography of a Yogi (Reprint of Original 1946 Edition)*. Crystal Clarity Publishers.

Yount, G., Church, D., Rachlin, K., Blickheuser, K., and Cardonna, I. (2019). Do Noncoding RNAs Mediate the Efficacy of Energy Psychology? *Global Advances in Health and Medicine*, 8, 216495611983250. https://doi.org/10.1177/2164956119832500

## Chapter 4

Coover, J. E. (1913). "The feeling of being stared at": Experimental. *The American Journal of Psychology*, *24*(4), 570–575. https://doi.org/10.2307/1413454

Fleming, M. A., Ehsan, L., Moore, S. R., and Levin, D. E. (2020). The Enteric Nervous System and Its Emerging Role as a Therapeutic Target. *Gastroenterology Research and Practice*, *2020*, 8024171. https://doi.org/10.1155/2020/8024171

Gershon, M. D., and Margolis, K. G. (2021). The gut, its microbiome, and the brain: Connections and communications. *The Journal of Clinical Investigation*, *131*(18), e143768. https://doi.org/10.1172/JCI143768

Mareschal, I., Calder, A. J., and Clifford, C. W. G. (2013). Humans have an expectation that gaze is directed toward them. *Current Biology: CB*, *23*(8), 717–721. https://doi.org/10.1016/j.cub.2013.03.030

Radin, D. I., and Schlitz, M. J. (2005). Gut feelings, intuition, and emotions: An exploratory study. *The Journal of Alternative and Complementary Medicine*, *11*(1), 85–91.

Schlitz, M., and LaBerge, S. (1997). Covert observation increases skin conductance in subjects unaware of when they are being observed: A replication. *Journal of Parapsychology*, *61*, 185–196.

Schlitz, M., Wiseman, R., Watt, C., and Radin, D. (2006). Of two minds: Sceptic-proponent collaboration within parapsychology. *British Journal of Psychology*, *97*(Pt 3), 313–322. https://doi.org/10.1348/000712605X80704

Sheldrake, R. (2000). The "sense of being stared at" does not depend on known sensory clues. *Rivista Di Biologia*, *93*(2), 237–252.

Sheldrake, R. (2005). The sense of being stared at – Part 1: Is it real or illusory? *Journal of Consciousness Studies*, *12*(6), 10–31.

Titchener, E. B. (1898). The "Feeling of Being Stared At." *Science (New York, N.Y.)*, *8*(208), 895–897. https://doi. org/10.1126/science.8.208.895

Tompkins, P., and Bird, C. (1989). *The Secret Life of Plants* (1st Printing edition). Harper and Row, Publishers.

Wiseman, R., and Smith, M. (1994). A further look at the detection of unseen gaze. *Proceedings of the Parapsychological Association 37th Annual Convention, Parapsychological Association*, 465–478.

## Part 2 introduction and Chapter 5

Bazley, C., Vink, P., Montgomery, J., and Hedge, A. (2016). Interior effects on comfort in healthcare waiting areas. *Work (Reading, Mass.)*, *54*(4), 791–806. https://doi. org/10.3233/WOR-162347

Charles, R., Glover, S., Bauchmüller, K., and Wood, D. (2017). Feng Shui and Emotional Response in the Critical Care Environment (FARCE) Study. *Anaesthesia*, *72*(12), 1528–1531. https://doi.org/10.1111/anae.14105

Ferrari, J. R., and Roster, C. A. (2018). Delaying Disposing: Examining the Relationship between Procrastination and Clutter across Generations. *Current Psychology*, *37*(2), 426–431. https://doi.org/10.1007/s12144-017-9679-4

Haughney, C. (2011). Before Move-In Day, Evicting the Old Auras. *New York Times.*

Jahn, R. G., Dunne, B. J., Nelson, R., Dobyns, Y. H., and Bradish, G. J. (2007). Correlations of random binary sequences with pre-stated operator intention: A review of a 12-year program. *Explore, 3*(3), 244–253.

Kay, A., Wheeler, S., Bargh, J., and Ross, L. (2004). Material priming: The influence of mundane physical objects on situational construal and competitive behavioral choice. *Organizational Behavior and Human Decision Processes, 95,* 83–96.

Kondo, M. (2014). *The Life-Changing Magic of Tidying Up: The Japanese Art of Decluttering and Organizing.* Ten Speed Press.

Minguillon, J., Lopez-Gordo, M. A., Renedo-Criado, D. A., Sanchez-Carrion, M. J., and Pelayo, F. (2017). Blue lighting accelerates post-stress relaxation: Results of a preliminary study. *PloS One, 12*(10), e0186399. https://doi.org/10.1371/journal.pone.0186399

Nelson, R. D., Radin, D. I., Shoup, R., and Bancel, P. (2002). Correlation of continuous random data with major world events. *Foundations of Physics Letters, 15*(6), 537–550.

Palmer, B. (2012). *Clutter Busting Your Life: Clearing Physical and Emotional Clutter to Reconnect with Yourself and Others.* New World Library.

Park, B. J., Tsunetsugu, Y., Kasetani, T., Kagawa, T., and Miyazaki, Y. (2010). The physiological effects of Shinrin-yoku (taking in the forest atmosphere or forest bathing): Evidence from field experiments in 24 forests across Japan. *Environmental Health and Preventive Medicine, 15*(1), 18–26. https://doi.org/10.1007/s12199-009-0086-9

Radin, D., Taft, R. J., and Yount, G. (2004). Effects of healing intention on cultured cells and truly random events. *The Journal of Alternative and Complementary Medicine*, *10*(1), 103–112. https://doi.org/10.1089/107555304322849020

Savani, K., Kumar, S., Naidu, N. V. R., and Dweck, C. S. (2011). Beliefs about emotional residue: The idea that emotions leave a trace in the physical environment. *Journal of Personality and Social Psychology*, *101*(4), 684–701. https://doi.org/10.1037/a0024102

Saxbe, D., and Repetti, R. L. (2010). No Place Like Home: Home Tours Correlate With Daily Patterns of Mood and Cortisol. *Phi Delta Kappan*, *36*(1), 25–28.

Singh, S. (2006). Impact of color on marketing. *Management Decision*, *44*(6), 783–789. https://doi.org/10.1108/00251740610673332

Taft, R., Moore, D., and Yount, G. (2005). Time-lapse analysis of potential cellular responsiveness to Johrei, a Japanese healing technique. *BMC Complementary and Alternative Medicine*, *5*, 2. https://doi.org/10.1186/1472-6882-5-2

Taft, R., Nieto, L., Luu, T., Pennucci, A., Moore, D., and Yount, G. (2005). Cultured Human Brain Tumor Cells Do Not Respond to Johrei Treatment. *Subtle Energies and Energy Medicine*, *14*(3), 253–265.

Tiller, W. A., Dibble Jr, W. E., Shealy, C. N., and Nunley, R. N. (2004). Toward general experimentation and discovery in conditioned laboratory spaces: Part II. pH-change experience at four remote sites, 1 year later. *The Journal of Alternative and Complementary Medicine*, *10*(2), 301–306.

## Chapter 6

Baker, J. O., and Bader, C. D. (2014). A social anthropology of ghosts in twenty-first-century America. *Social Compass, 61*(4), 569–593. https://doi.org/10.1177/0037768614547337

BBC News. (2002, May 26). Cannes film sickens audience. *BBC.* http://news.bbc.co.uk/2/hi/entertainment/2008796.stm

Booth, J. N., Koren, S. A., and Persinger, M. A. (2005). Increased feelings of the sensed presence and increased geomagnetic activity at the time of the experience during exposures to transcerebral weak complex magnetic fields. *The International Journal of Neuroscience, 115*(7), 1053–1079. https://doi.org/10.1080/00207450590901521

Chaban, R., Ghazy, A., Georgiade, E., Stumpf, N., and Vahl, C.-F. (2021). Negative Effect of High-Level Infrasound on Human Myocardial Contractility: In-Vitro Controlled Experiment. *Noise and Health, 23*(109), 57–66. www.ncbi.nlm.nih.gov/pmc/articles/PMC8411947/

Cook, C. M., and Persinger, M. A. (1997). Experimental induction of the "sensed presence" in normal subjects and an exceptional subject. *Perceptual and Motor Skills, 85*(2), 683–693. https://doi.org/10.2466/pms.1997.85.2.683

Dagnall, N., Drinkwater, K. G., O'Keeffe, C., Ventola, A., Laythe, B., Jawer, M. A., Massullo, B., Caputo, G. B., and Houran, J. (2020). Things That Go Bump in the Literature: An Environmental Appraisal of "Haunted Houses." *Frontiers in Psychology, 11.* https://doi.org/10.3389/fpsyg.2020.01328

# REFERENCES

Jacobi, K. P. (2003). *The Malevolent "Undead":
Cross-Cultural Perspectives.* 96–109. https://doi.
org/10.4135/9781412914291.n11

Lange, R., and Houran, J. (1997). Context-induced
paranormal experiences: Support for Houran and Lange's
model of haunting phenomena. *Perceptual and Motor
Skills, 84*(3 Pt 2), 1455–1458. https://doi.org/10.2466/
pms.1997.84.3c.1455

Lange, R., Houran, J., Harte, T. M., and Havens, R. A. (1996).
Contextual mediation of perceptions in hauntings and
poltergeist-like experiences. *Perceptual and Motor
Skills, 82*(3 Pt 1), 755–762. https://doi.org/10.2466/
pms.1996.82.3.755

Meli, S. C., and Persinger, M. A. (2009). Red light facilitates
the sensed presence elicited by application of weak,
burst-firing magnetic fields over the temporal lobes. *The
International Journal of Neuroscience, 119*(1), 68–75.
https://doi.org/10.1080/00207450802507689

Persinger, M. A. (1993). Vectorial cerebral hemisphericity
as differential sources for the sensed presence, mystical
experiences and religious conversions. *Perceptual and
Motor Skills, 76*(3 Pt 1), 915–930. https://doi.org/10.2466/
pms.1993.76.3.915

Poppy, C. (2017, March 27). *A scientific approach to the
paranormal.* https://www.ted.com/talks/carrie_poppy_a_
scientific_approach_to_the_paranormal

Schneider, F. (1913). An Investigation of a "Haunted" House.
*Science (New York, N.Y.), 37*(958), 711–712. https://doi.
org/10.1126/science.37.958.711

Stierwalt, S. (2019, February 5). *6 Possible Scientific Reasons for Ghosts. Scientific American.* https://www. scientificamerican.com/article/6-possible-scientific-reasons-for-ghosts/

St-Pierre, L. S., and Persinger, M. A. (2006). Experimental facilitation of the sensed presence is predicted by the specific patterns of the applied magnetic fields, not by suggestibility: Re-analyses of 19 experiments. *The International Journal of Neuroscience, 116*(9), 1079–1096. https://doi.org/10.1080/00207450600808800

Tandy, V., and Lawrence, T. (1998). The Ghost in the Machine. *Journal of the Society for Psychical Research, 62,* 851.

Tandy, V., and Lawrence, T. (2004, November). Bid to find Evidence of Ghosts at Castle. *Coventry Evening Telegraph.*

Wiseman, R. (2008). *Quirkology: How We Discover the Big Truths in Small Things* (Illustrated edition). Basic Books.

Wiseman, R., Watt, C., Greening, E., Stevens, P., and O'Keefe, C. (2002). An investigation into the alleged haunting of Hampton Court Palace: Psychological variables and magnetic fields. *Journal of Parapsychology, 66,* 387–408.

## Chapter 7

Hale, S. E., and Campbell, D. (2007). *Sacred Space, Sacred Sound: The Acoustic Mysteries of Holy Places.* Quest Books.

Till, R. (2019). Sound Archaeology: A Study of the Acoustics of Three World Heritage Sites, Spanish Prehistoric Painted

Caves, Stonehenge, and Paphos Theatre. *Acoustics, 1*(3), Article 3. https://doi.org/10.3390/acoustics1030039

Tolle, E. (1997). *The Power of Now: A Guide to Spiritual Enlightenment.* Namaste Press

## Chapter 8 and Final Words

Alfonso-Goldfarb, A. M., and Jubran, S. A. C. (2008). Listening to the whispers of matter through Arabic hermeticism: New studies on the *Book of the Treasure of Alexander. Ambix, 55*(2), 99–121. https://doi.org/10.1179/174582308X255426

Bratman, G. N., Hamilton, J. P., Hahn, K. S., Daily, G. C., and Gross, J. J. (2015). Nature experience reduces rumination and subgenual prefrontal cortex activation. *Proceedings of the National Academy of Sciences of the United States of America, 112*(28), 8567–8572. https://doi.org/10.1073/pnas.1510459112

Carhart-Harris, R. L., Bolstridge, M., Rucker, J., Day, C. M. J., Erritzoe, D., Kaelen, M., Bloomfield, M., Rickard, J. A., Forbes, B., Feilding, A., Taylor, D., Pilling, S., Curran, V. H., and Nutt, D. J. (2016). Psilocybin with psychological support for treatment-resistant depression: An open-label feasibility study. *The Lancet. Psychiatry, 3*(7), 619–627. https://doi.org/10.1016/S2215-0366(16)30065-7

Chamberlin, K., Smith, W., Chirgwin, C., Appasani, S., and Rioux, P. (2014). Analysis of the charge exchange between the human body and ground: Evaluation of "earthing" from an electrical perspective. *Journal of Chiropractic Medicine, 13*(4), 239–246. https://doi.org/10.1016/j.jcm.2014.10.001

Chevalier, G., Sinatra, S. T., Oschman, J. L., Sokal, K., and Sokal, P. (2012). Earthing: Health implications of reconnecting the human body to the Earth's surface electrons. *Journal of Environmental and Public Health*, *2012*, 291541. https://doi.org/10.1155/2012/291541

Davis, A. K., Barrett, F. S., May, D. G., Cosimano, M. P., Sepeda, N. D., Johnson, M. W., Finan, P. H., and Griffiths, R. R. (2021). Effects of Psilocybin-Assisted Therapy on Major Depressive Disorder: A Randomized Clinical Trial. *JAMA Psychiatry*, *78*(5), 481–489. https://doi.org/10.1001/jamapsychiatry.2020.3285

Gale, L., Vedhara, K., Searle, A., Kemple, T., and Campbell, R. (2008). Patients' perspectives on foot complications in type 2 diabetes: A qualitative study. *The British Journal of General Practice*, *58*(553), 555–563. https://doi.org/10.3399/bjgp08X319657

Griffiths, R. R., Johnson, M. W., Carducci, M. A., Umbricht, A., Richards, W. A., Richards, B. D., Cosimano, M. P., and Klinedinst, M. A. (2016). Psilocybin produces substantial and sustained decreases in depression and anxiety in patients with life-threatening cancer: A randomized double-blind trial. *Journal of Psychopharmacology (Oxford, England)*, *30*(12), 1181–1197. https://doi.org/10.1177/0269881116675513

Grob, C. S., Danforth, A. L., Chopra, G. S., Hagerty, M., McKay, C. R., Halberstadt, A. L., and Greer, G. R. (2011). Pilot study of psilocybin treatment for anxiety in patients with advanced-stage cancer. *Archives of General Psychiatry*, *68*(1), 71–78. https://doi.org/10.1001/archgenpsychiatry.2010.116

Haijen, E. C. H. M., Kaelen, M., Roseman, L., Timmermann, C., Kettner, H., Russ, S., Nutt, D., Daws, R. E., Hampshire, A. D. G., Lorenz, R., and Carhart-Harris, R. L. (2018). Predicting Responses to Psychedelics: A Prospective Study. *Frontiers in Pharmacology*, *9*, 897. https://doi.org/10.3389/fphar.2018.00897

Harvey, M. L., Oskins, J. D., McCarter, K. N., and Baker, J. R. (2016). Direct Earth Contact: Barefootedness and Nature Connection. *Ecopsychology*, *8*(2), 96–106. https://doi.org/10.1089/eco.2015.0075

Hill, N. (2005). *Think and Grow Rich*. TarcherPerigee.

Hutcherson, C. A., Seppala, E. M., and Gross, J. J. (2008). Loving-kindness meditation increases social connectedness. *Emotion*, *8*(5), 720–724. https://doi.org/10.1037/a0013237

King, V. (2018). *Good Vibes, Good Life: How Self-Love Is the Key to Unlocking Your Greatness* (Illustrated edition). Hay House UK.

Kotera, Y., Richardson, M., and Sheffield, D. (2022). Effects of Shinrin-Yoku (forest bathing) and Nature Therapy on Mental Health: A Systematic Review and Meta-analysis. *International Journal of Mental Health and Addiction*, *20*(1), 337–361. https://doi.org/10.1007/s11469-020-00363-4

Leary, T., Litwin, G. H., and Metzner, R. (1963). Reactions to psilocybin administered in a supportive environment. *The Journal of Nervous and Mental Disease*, *137*, 561–573. https://doi.org/10.1097/00005053-196312000-00007

Li, Q. (2010). Effect of forest bathing trips on human immune function. *Environmental Health and Preventive Medicine*, *15*(1), 9–17. https://doi.org/10.1007/s12199-008-0068-3

Lowe, H., Toyang, N., Steele, B., Valentine, H., Grant, J., Ali, A., Ngwa, W., and Gordon, L. (2021). The Therapeutic Potential of Psilocybin. *Molecules (Basel, Switzerland)*, *26*(10), 2948. https://doi.org/10.3390/molecules26102948

Marzetti, L., Di Lanzo, C., Zappasodi, F., Chella, F., Raffone, A., and Pizzella, V. (2014). Magnetoencephalographic alpha band connectivity reveals differential default mode network interactions during focused attention and open monitoring meditation. *Frontiers in Human Neuroscience*, *8*, 832. https://doi.org/10.3389/fnhum.2014.00832

Piff, P. K., Dietze, P., Feinberg, M., Stancato, D. M., and Keltner, D. (2015). Awe, the small self, and prosocial behavior. *Journal of Personality and Social Psychology*, *108*(6), 883–899. https://doi.org/10.1037/pspi0000018

Pollan, M. (2018). *How To Change Your Mind*. Penguin Press.

Preller, K. H., Duerler, P., Burt, J. B., Ji, J. L., Adkinson, B., Stämpfli, P., Seifritz, E., Repovš, G., Krystal, J. H., Murray, J. D., Anticevic, A., and Vollenweider, F. X. (2020). Psilocybin Induces Time-Dependent Changes in Global Functional Connectivity. *Biological Psychiatry*, *88*(2), 197–207. https://doi.org/10.1016/j.biopsych.2019.12.027

Raffone, A., Marzetti, L., Del Gratta, C., Perrucci, M. G., Romani, G. L., and Pizzella, V. (2019). Toward a brain theory of meditation. *Progress in Brain Research*, *244*, 207–232. https://doi.org/10.1016/bs.pbr.2018.10.028

Ravinder, J., Barnes, Vernon A. and Crawford, M. W. (2014). Mind-Body Response and Neurophysiological changes during stress and Meditation: Central Role of Homeostasis. *Journal of Biological Regulators and Homeostatic Agents* 28 (4):545-554.

# REFERENCES

Ross, S., Bossis, A., Guss, J., Agin-Liebes, G., Malone, T.,
Cohen, B., Mennenga, S. E., Belser, A., Kalliontzi, K.,
Babb, J., Su, Z., Corby, P., and Schmidt, B. L. (2016). Rapid
and sustained symptom reduction following psilocybin
treatment for anxiety and depression in patients with life-
threatening cancer: A randomized controlled trial. *Journal
of Psychopharmacology (Oxford, England), 30*(12),
1165–1180. https://doi.org/10.1177/0269881116675512

Yuen, H. K., and Jenkins, G. R. (2020). Factors associated with
changes in subjective well-being immediately after urban
park visit. *International Journal of Environmental Health
Research, 30*(2), 134–145. https://doi.org/10.1080/096031
23.2019.1577368

# FURTHER RESOURCES

Institute of Noetic Sciences Blog: Frontier research, noetic practices & events. https://noetic.org/blog/

## Books

*Beyond Goodbye: An Extraordinary Story of a Shared Death Experience* by Annie Cap. Paragon Publishing, 2011.

*The Biology of Belief* by Bruce Lipton. Mountain of Love/Elite Books, 2005.

*Clutter Busting Your Life: Clearing Physical and Emotional Clutter to Reconnect with Yourself and Others* by Brooks Palmer. New World Library, 2012.

*Entangled Minds* by Dean Radin. Pocket Books, 2006.

*Extraordinary Knowing: Science, Skepticism, and the Inexplicable Powers of the Human Mind* by Elizabeth Lloyd Mayer. Bantam, 2008.

*From Outer Space to Inner Space: An Apollo Astronaut's Journey Through the Material and Mystical Worlds* by Edgar Mitchell. Red Wheel/Weiser, 2023.

*How to Change Your Mind* by Michael Pollan. Penguin Books, 2019.

*I and Thou* by Martin Buber. T. & T. Clark, 1937.

*Jacob Atabet: A Speculative Fiction* by Michael Murphy. Celestial Arts, 1977.

*The Life-Changing Magic of Tidying Up* by Marie Kondo. Vermilion, 2014.

*Real Magic: Ancient Wisdom, Modern Science, and a Guide to the Secret Power of the Universe* by Dean Radin. Harmony, 2018.

*The Power of Now* by Eckhart Tolle. New World Library, 1999.

*The Sense of Being Stared At* by Rupert Sheldrake. Park Street Press, 2013.

*Spiritual Ecology: The Cry of the Earth* edited by Llewellyn Vaughan-Lee. The Golden Sufi Center, 2016.

*Urban Tantra, Second Edition: Sacred Sex for the Twenty-First Century* by Barbara Carrellas. Ten Speed Press, 2007.

# Podcasts and TED Talks

*Mind and Life* podcast with Jon Kabat-Zinn

*A Scientific Approach to the Paranormal.* TED talk by Carrie Poppy

*Step into Magic* podcast with Josephine Liang

*White Shores* podcast with Theresa Cheung

# About Us

Welbeck Balance publishes books dedicated to changing lives. Our mission is to deliver life-enhancing books to help improve your wellbeing so that you can live your life with greater clarity and meaning, wherever you are on life's journey.

Welbeck Balance is part of the Welbeck Publishing Group – a globally recognized independent publisher. Welbeck are renowned for our innovative ideas, production values and developing long-lasting content. Our books have been translated into over 30 languages in more than 60 countries around the world.

If you love books, then join the club and sign up to our newsletter for exclusive offers, extracts, author interviews and more information.

**www.welbeckpublishing.com**

welbeckpublish
welbeckpublish
welbeckuk

# NOTES

# NOTES

# NOTES

# NOTES

# NOTES

# NOTES